The
Sacred Sex
Bible

MW00695781

The
Sacred Sex
Bible

A guide to sex and spirit in the East and West

Cassandra Lorius

FIREFLY BOOKS

A FIREFLY BOOK

Published by Firefly Books Ltd. 2011

Copyright © Octopus Publishing Group Ltd 2011
Text copyright © Cassandra Lorius

All rights reserved. No part of this publication may be
reproduced, stored in a retrieval system, or transmitted
in any form or by any means, electronic, mechanical,
photocopying, recording or otherwise, without the prior
written permission of the Publisher.

First printing

Publisher Cataloging-in-Publication Data (U.S.)
Lorius, Cassandra.
   The sacred sex bible : a guide to sex and spirit in the east
and west / Cassandra Lorius.
[400] p. : col. photos. ; cm.
Includes index.
Summary: Guide to sex and spirituality, including: historical
and cultural currents in sexuality, the influence of Western and
Eastern traditions, and examples of sexual practice and rituals.
ISBN-13: 978-1-55407-947-6 (pbk.)
1. Sex. 2. Sex and history. 3. Sex customs.
4. Sex--Religious aspects. I. Title.
306.7 dc22   GN484.3L675   2011

Library and Archives Canada Cataloguing in Publication
A CIP record of this book is available from Library and
Archives Canada

Published in the United States by
Firefly Books (U.S.) Inc.
P.O. Box 1338, Ellicott Station
Buffalo, New York 14205

Published in Canada by
Firefly Books Ltd.
66 Leek Crescent
Richmond Hill, Ontario L4B 1H1

Printed in Hong Kong

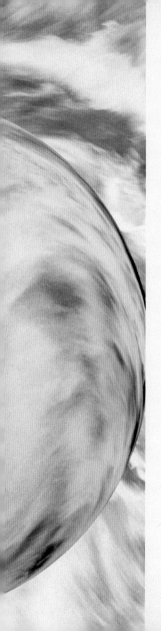

Contents

Introduction

Sacred sexuality is a powerful concept that has endured for millennia. The idea brings together two primal motivating forces within us, establishing that something so primal – sex – can also be deeply satisfying on the more profound levels of our being.

Sex and the sacred in the modern era have for the most part been separated and opposed, particularly with the rise of monotheistic religions and throughout the Christian era. In contemporary culture sex is treated as anything but sacred. In fact, it can be considered sacrilegious to use the language of the sacred in relation to the passions of the body.

The notion that sex is about little more than physical gratification severely limits the capacity that it offers for exploring a more profound connection between two people. While, as a practising sex therapist, I agree that it's good to develop love-making techniques, the focus of most self-help books on achieving satisfactory orgasm ignores the other levels of experience – emotional and even spiritual – that

Goddess figurines such as this Ancient Egyptian icon of Isis are found across the ancient world in Africa and Asia.

The development of sacred sexuality begins with re-establishing the archetypal figure of the goddess, and reclaiming her within your own relationships.

great sex can offer. Descriptions of sexual satisfaction are not shy of using terms like 'heavenly' and 'blissful' – qualities often connected to deep, respectful and appreciative partnerships, in which trust between lovers is paramount.

There is a great desire in contemporary society to reclaim the 'holy' and make love-making truly divine. In making love with a sense of the sacred, your body becomes a temple and your partner's body a shrine. You use your bodies to worship one another and sex becomes a means of opening up to the sacred dimensions of life as a whole. In sacred sex, touch becomes precious; sounds and smells heighten your sensitivity and sensuality. The world of the senses intensifies your connection creating a shared experience as well as a mutual inter-dependence. Tried and tested techniques associated with spiritual awakening, such as yogic breath and vizualisation, are incorporated into love-making to create a multi-dimensional experience of sex as communion.

What is sacred sex?

Physicists and mystics alike are united in describing the universe as a dynamic field of vibrating energy, and practitioners of sacred sex call this field of energy 'bliss'. Regardless of their religious affiliation, many people describe the ecstasy that can arise out of deeply bonded love-making as a mystical union, which creates a lasting sense of oneness or peace in its wake. Among sacred sex practitioners, bliss describes a way of experiencing reality, rather than a goal of sex and orgasm.

Sacred sex refers to both the context and the content of sex: couples approach their bodies as a temple permeated with the divine and their sexual union as a sacred form of union. They celebrate love-making and may see it as a gateway to blissful communion, in which they meet the divine in one another. These couples may choose to work at their relationships until there is a level of awareness, appreciation and trust that allows them to go deeper in exploring their sexuality. Other couples seek out and use techniques gleaned from older traditions, in which ritual sex was part of a different, and perhaps more personal, understanding of the realm of the sacred. Trying out such techniques

These 13th century Indian Maithuna erotic figures are fine examples of erotic statuary found in temples throughout Asia.

can offer a glimpse of sex as something much more satisfying than past experience may have provided, and this can inspire couples to explore sacred sex traditions. As we shall see in this book, such ideas have been around since the beginning of human history.

The notion of reverence in the realm of sexuality might seem like a new-age phenomenon, but the roots of sacred sex stretch back into the earliest history of humanity, where the worship of the divine was not separate from the realm of nature, including the processes and cycles that link and separate the material and spiritual realms. Goddesses were probably also metaphors for core aspects of cosmic consciousness – the idea that the universe is an interconnected network, with each conscious being linked to every other – as opposed to our individual, temporal, human identity. Goddess worship was doubtless about more than guaranteeing the ongoing fertility of nature in early agrarian communities, although ensuring the harvest was, of course, key to survival, for if crops were abundant, the community would flourish. Among Neolithic and Paleolithic cultures, an aspect of goddess worship appears to have been worship of nature and the propitiation of nature spirits in plants and the natural environment, along with mysteries of sex and the relationship between female and male principles.

Sex and society

Because our own culture too often treats sex as either prosaic or profane, it may be hard to imagine how it could once have been central to a culture in which sexuality was a defining feature of the Goddess. However, these early beliefs appear to have survived in the form of present-day Tantric teachings and practices within the Indian traditions.

The mystics of Eastern traditions, in which sacred sex has played a crucial part, were remarkable in using sexual rites as a pathway to a deeper form of ecstasy, seen as the goal of spiritual awakening (see page 176).

Our ideas about religion and sexuality reflect the kind of society in which we find ourselves living, where for thousands of years the majority of people have tended to channel anything we might call 'spiritual' into established religious forms of expression. Mystical traditions throughout the millennia, whether as trends within mainstream religions or as discrete cults, have emphasized personal experience as the gateway to a more personal relationship with the divine. Over diverse areas and historical periods, many sects and groups of practitioners appear to have explored religion through direct experience in ways that were not included or recorded by mainstream religions. Once religious hierarchies became established, they tended to repress difference or dissent in their need to consolidate their power. The majority of these sects were successfully wiped out, especially in Europe.

For the last few thousand years, the dominant world religions have largely treated sexuality as a distraction from the spiritual path. Christian saints were ideally celibate, and in his hugely influential 4th century autobiographical *Confessions*, Augustine decried relationships with women as the ultimate distraction – despite his 15-year relationship with a concubine, with whom he fathered a son. Augustine cemented the split between sexuality and spirituality that characterized mainstream Christianity, which was to become much more severe over the next two millennia. In embracing the freedom from social pressures offered by a celibate lifestyle, he went much further, positioning sex as a fundamental

We do not need to recreate complex rites and ritualistic practices from other times and places, but can use them to learn and grow.

barrier to spiritual freedom. He characterized the conflict between sex and sexuality as 'the lust of the flesh against the spirit'. This was a radical shift from the broadly positive attitudes towards sexuality among pagans and Jews that had existed until a couple of centuries after the death of Christ.

The Sacred Sex Bible examines historical and cultural currents in sexuality and the influence of other traditions incorporating ritual sex. Scholar Howard Urban refers to the current new-age tendency to mine Tantric traditions, creating a version of sacred sex that is stripped of religious and cultural baggage, as a re-imagining of such practices. By the same token many practitioners in India and Tibet also engage in re-imagining some of the rituals of their own traditions.

Even if rituals have great antiquity, in using them for personal practice we inevitably customize them and reshape them to our own needs. This book provides an imagined exploration of sacred sex, while drawing on some of the research and thoughts of philosophers and academics, as well as contemporary teachers of sacred sex.

Inside *The Sacred Sex Bible*

Chapter 1, Goddess Worship from the Ancients to the Alchemists, explores early goddess worship, high priestesses as sexual initiators, rites in ancient Greece and Hermetic beliefs inspired by Hellenistic and Egyptian writings. The great goddess was represented as Lover, Mother, Daughter, Sister, Wisdom and Holy Spirit, providing an image of the Divine Feminine reflected at the human level. Spiritual practice may have incorporated sexual rites as a potent means of accessing wisdom and we look at the persistence of sacred rites and the inspirational power of goddesses, or the priestesses and sybils who stood in for these goddesses. The emerging theme is the spiritual belief in the perfectibility of the person – through union between men and women and the union of earthly with divine.

Chapter 2, The Sacred Feminine in Christian Traditions, illuminates the central importance of the figure of Wisdom from pre-Christian traditions, which was incorporated into the early Christian sects known as Gnostics. The figures of Sophia, Eve, Lilith and the serpent, and the Judaic mystical tradition of Caballa are all examined. In the early centuries of Christianity notions of piety and chastity led to unusual practices, possibly inspired by the age-old institution of the hieros gamos, or sacred marriage ritual, in which the sexual union of mother and father gods was reenacted.

Chapter 3, Western Thinking: Sin, Sex and Freud, examines aspects of sexuality in the West from the Middle Ages through the Victorian era, and the rise of the medical model of sexuality that is influential today to Freud and Jung who brought psychological thinking into the mainstream.

In Chapter 4, Eastern Approaches to Sex and the Spirit, we see how modern physics offers us a world view that has much in common with ancient Eastern traditions, and we look at the ways in which bliss is defined. We explore the spiritual paths of yoga, meditation and the Hindu, Buddhist and Daoist traditions, and look at the importance of techniques such as mindfulness and the role of subtle energy bodies (such as the chakra system) in awakening sexual energy.

Chapter 5, Tantra Deities and Practices, explores the ways in which Tantric strands within Hinduism and Buddhism incorporate unique methods to achieve union with the divine and remind us of the sacredness of sexuality. We look at the practices and deities associated with Tantra and the influence of dynamic forms of meditation and sexual freedom, spawning the current popularity of Tantra.

Chapter 6, Making Sex Sacred, looks at the ways in which sacred sex traditions can be incorporated into your own relationship, offering techniques for cultivating compassion, presence and good communication, as well as explicit sexual practices drawn from Neo-Tantra (or Tantra in the West), which expand your awareness of the sacred in sex to open the doorway to ecstasy.

The glossary explains some of the terms used in discussions of sacred sexuality and their derivation in the original Sanskrit, Tibetan and Greek. It can be referred to when reading the book.

Goddess Worship
from the Ancients
to the Alchemists

Goddess worship in prehistoric times

Deities fitting the modern conception of the mother goddess have been revered from the Paleolithic and Neolithic eras onwards, across a wide range of cultures. Today, modern pagans, witches and other New Age movements thrive in the West. From Egyptian Isis to Gaia among the ancient Greeks and the Andean goddess Pacha Mama, there is plentiful evidence of ritual life that treats relations between people as a mirror of each culture's earliest creation myths. Through goddess worship, women had the opportunity to see themselves reflected in their role as mothers and guardians of creation (and its fruits).

In many ancient cultures, goddesses were revered as earth mothers – as we can see from clay figurines depicting ample women with birth-worn bellies, child-bearing hips and protruding genitals.

The Venus of Willendorf, a famous fertility figure dating from c. 23,000 BCE, which is assumed to have been used for goddess worship.

An image of Pacha Mama, a South American Mother Earth, has been painted on the Wall of Peace, in Santiago, Chile, inspiring contemporary artists who reject violence in favour of disarmament.

These figurines appear to be icons, which may have been used in worship of the sacred power of women. Women were associated with the magic and mystery of fertility and childbirth, and some of these figures may have been used in magical ways (see page 52). The mysteries of giving birth and women's role in nurturing and sustaining life and relationships were awe inspiring. There are widespread findings of earth goddess figurines in communities that valued and relied upon the fecundity of earth, as society moved from hunter-gatherer forms of social organization to settled communities where crops were cultivated.

Fertility rituals

Early goddess worship was also concerned with maintaining the fertility of the land so that the community could survive. Rituals were connected with encouraging abundant harvests and renewing the storehouse each summer, which held the community grain so vital for the winter.

Recorded history generally starts with the Sumerian civilization of ancient Iraq (circa 3000 BCE), although earlier temples such as the Ggantija temples on Gozo, Malta, provide evidence that feminized forms of worship predated the rise of Sumer.

Sumer was situated along the river Tigris and stretched from the coast up to Baghdad, in modern-day Iraq. Sumer was a desert region,

although it was probably more verdant then than now. Some of the ritual verse dedicated to the great goddess Inanna (see page 24) is concerned with invoking the fertility of the land, naming a number of different plants, as well as animals and fish. Many plants were probably used in early ritual.

These terracotta figurines of naked women had a ritual purpose, used in Mesopotamia (modern day Southern Iraq) 1900–1300 BCE.

The Seated Woman of Çatal Höyük, giving birth on her throne. Leopards, lions and other powerful animals figure in early depictions of the goddess.

Harmonious relations between the nurturing mother and undomesticated animals and birds were also extremely important attributes of the (Sumerian) Lady of the Beasts and early bird goddesses.

Goddess of Çatal Höyük

One key piece of evidence for goddess culture was found at Çatal Höyük in Anatolia (now in eastern Turkey), a Neolithic settlement dating from 6500 BCE, which was home to a population of between five and ten thousand. The famous Seated Woman (above) was found in a grain bin, which led excavations director James Mellaart to believe that it was connected with ensuring the harvest.

The social organization of early cultures

There is still debate about whether these societies were matriarchal, dominated by women, or egalitarian, with women and men considered as equals. This is partly because such cultures existed before the development of complex forms of writing, and also because archaeologists have to make inferences based on whatever remains are uncovered, which can be influenced by their own theories and assumptions.

With the influence of feminist scholarship, until fairly recently it was fashionable to assume that earliest society was matriarchal until it was gradually eroded by the ascendancy of masculine power structures. More recent research suggests that social organization in the ancient world was likely to have been matrifocal, with goddess worship pre-dominating but without women lording it over men. Chief among these researchers is archaeologist Marija Gimbutas, who grounds her

Early representations of women were of fecund mother goddesses with childbearing hips and prominent genitals.

writing about the goddess culture of Old Europe in a close examination of the archaeological record. She believes that the move from hunter-gathering modes of existence to settled crop cultivation, which marked the beginning of the Neolithic period around 10,000 BCE, created social groupings centred on the worship of nature and local goddesses.

Holistic theory

Gimbutas developed a style of 'mytho-archaeological' theorizing, drawing on other disciplines such as linguistics, ethnology, folklore and historical records in order to

Birds and animals were honoured throughout antiquity, and aligned with goddesses such as Sophia, as nature and the spirit world were seen as one.

reimagine prehistoric civilizations. After excavating several major sites, she concluded that symbolism in the early civilization of pre-history is based on an understanding that life is in eternal transformation and constant rhythmic change between creation and destruction, birth and death. She says, 'The concept of regeneration and renewal is the most ... dramatic theme.' Mythical thought appears to her to be imbued with the sacred and a powerful motivation towards intimate participation with the cyclic processes of fertility/birth, death and regeneration.

This 1702 engraving of the Phrygian goddess Cybele, worshipped from ancient times as Kubaba, shows her wearing a crown of towers originally representing her Babylonian temples.

A flowering of spiritual life was apparent in the art of these prehistoric cultures. Domestic and creative works and the notable absence of weaponry point to a long period of peaceable life; there is also evidence of an early sacred script and sophisticated crafts, as well as a large number of female figurines described as mother goddess types – with clear ritual use. Gimbutas found no evidence of a great father god, nor are there sculptures of a sacred couple in this early period. Investigating the remains of habitations in a number of sites throughout Europe of that period, Marija Gimbutas notes that it is striking that houses were all of a similar size, which suggests that there was no privileged ruling class. Male and female skeletons, too, were of similar size, which points to the fact that men and women had the same nutritional status.

From excavations at various sites (Çatal Höyük, the Ukraine and Moldovia), temples containing numerous clay figurines in the style of recognized goddesses such as the Magna Mater found in Malta, and from a study of Neolithic symbols demonstrating that the female form was associated with creation, Gimbutas suggests that these societies consisted of a temple community guided by a queen priestess, with a brother or uncle as consort and a council of women as a governing body.

From Mesopotamia across Old Europe and into the Scottish Highlands, these communities flourished until, around the 4th millennium BCE, they were overrun by Indo-Europeans known as Kurgans, who imposed a social order based on hunting and kingship. The rise of the warrior king developed a culture of the hero figure bent on a drive for conquest. This marked the beginning of the shift to patriarchal structures in Europe.

The principle of Eros

Jungian analyst Julian David believes that Eros (love), to borrow the term from the later Greeks, appears to have been a guiding principle in these communities, valuing our need for interdependence and the role of bringing opposites together. Eros had a wider and more holistic definition than the current one of sexual love, encompassing creativity and connectedness.

A rare and early representation of lovers, this Neolithic sculpture of an embracing couple, excavated at Çatal Höyük, is around 8,000 years old.

Inanna, 'Queen of Heaven and Earth'

Inanna is among the earliest-known great goddesses, from ancient Sumer, dating from at least around 3000 BCE. She was worshipped for a very long time, and the fragment of poetry opposite comes from the first detailed text celebrating her story. It suggests the style of sex rituals that may have been involved in her worship. According to the sentiments put in the mouth of Inanna, the goddess took great joy in sexual relations with her consort, and one might reasonably assume that sexual relations for some couples in Sumer celebrated sex as a mirror of the divine:

The 'Queen of the Night' relief, from an Old Babylonian shrine, 1800–1750 BCE, depicts either Inanna/ Ishtar, her underworld sister Ereshkigal, or Lilith.

> *I bathed for the wild bull*
> *I bathed for the Shepherd Dumuzi*
> *I perfumed my sides with ointment*
> *I coated my mouth with sweet-smelling amber*
> *I painted my eyes with kohl.*
>
> *He shaped my loins with his fair hands*
> *The Shepherd Dumuzi filled my lap*
> *with cream and milk*
> *He stroked my pubic hair*
> *He watered my womb*
> *He laid his hands on my holy vulva*
> *The quick end to my narrowboat with milk*
> *He confessed to me on the bed.*
>
> *Now I will caress my high priest on the bed*
> *I will caress the faithful Shepherd Dumuzi*
> *I will caress his loins, the Shepherdship of the land*
> *I will decree a sweet fate to him.*

Inanna, Queen of Heaven and Earth
Translation by Diane Wolkstein and Samuel Kramer

The practice of ritual sacred sex between a female goddess and her consort appears to have lasted for thousands of years, even into biblical times. Most of the remnants of such practices had come to an end by the time the emperor Constantine reconsecrated the last of the goddess temples in the 4th century CE and replaced them with Christian churches.

25

Sacred marriage

Later commentators describe sexual rituals in both Sumer and Babylonia as modelled on the hieros gamos, or 'sacred marriage', between a king and a high priestess of Inanna. The high priestess would choose for her bed a young man who represented the shepherd Dumuzi (later called Tammuz), consort of Inanna, in the sacred marriage, celebrated during the annual (New Year) ceremony, at the spring equinox.

For the duration of the ritual the young man became Inanna's consort, in order to share in her potency, and perhaps her divinity. Unfortunately, no text tells us what happened in the temple's ritual bed, but the language used for all such rituals is deeply erotic.

Sacred possession

As Inanna, the human identity of the priestess would have been largely irrelevant. Speculating on the basis of what we know about the widespread practise of incubation (entering trance in order to access ritual knowledge) in the later Near East, such rituals probably occurred during trance states, in which the goddess was believed to literally inhabit the priestess, while her partner, usually a high-status community leader, embodied Inanna's beloved Dumuzi. Later examples of ritual trance include the oracular priestesses accorded great status through whom Apollo spoke at Delphi and the Dionysian Maenad.

Ancient Mesopotamia, like most other cultures, had its prophets and seers who commonly used trance to reach ecstatic states. Looking at the practice of sacred sex from this perspective, the goddess Inanna would

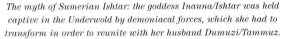

The myth of Sumerian Ishtar: the goddess Inanna/Ishtar was held captive in the Underwold by demoniacal forces, which she had to transform in order to reunite with her husband Dumuzi/Tammuz.

have been seen to be using the body of a devout ecstatic and priestess, rather than a priestess impersonating her, and the priestess would have been accorded high status and reverence for her role.

In these early civilizations, sacred marriage appears to have been an organizing principle, where the high priestess, invested with the presence of the divine, took as her consort a mortal, her chosen beloved, in a marriage of heaven and earth. The priestess represented the eternal, while the mortal man, who would symbolically die, may have been replaced in spring at the start of the New Year.

Temple sex

Mesopotamian priestesses of ancient Babylonia and Sumer were cultivated women, part of whose role may have been to initiate men into the mysteries of the goddess through sex. This intriguing idea is suggested by the ancient Greek historian Herodotus (440 BCE). As worship involves accepting, honouring and nourishing the more subtle dimensions of human experience and acting as witness to the way the sacred operates in the human realm, participating in sacred rituals had the potential to divinize the human experience. By the time of Herodotus, however, this sacred experience seems to have become trivialized, as he refers to such rituals as taking place with prostitutes. In an openly derogatory tone, he wrote that, 'The foulest Babylonian custom'

Ancient Roman erotic relief sculpture depicting Psyche with her immortal lover Amor.

This fresco from the Hall of the Mysteries, Pompeii, depicts a Dionysian initiate weeping while a bacchante dances.

compelled 'every woman of the land to sit in the temple of Aphrodite and have intercourse with some stranger once in her life' ...

Sacred rites

While Herodotus claimed sacred 'prostitution' was common practice in the ancient Near East and described many 'houses of heaven', little evidence has been found to support his claims. Other scholars suggest that he may simply have been unable to imagine any role for women in ritual life that did not involve sexual intercourse. Even if ancient priestesses practised ritual sex, and also received offerings for the temples, they would not have been considered prostitutes in the way we would use the term today. Sex is not just about the act itself: it's also about connecting to another and, through this contact, cultivating a more collaborative awareness and creating and strengthening bonds. The kinds of bonds created through sexual ritual depend on the shared world view held by the participants – which remains true today. We make of sex what we imagine it to be.

The Whore of Babylon

In contemporary popular culture, Babylon is synonymous with a degenerate culture that had passed its prime. In describing the coming Apocalypse, Revelation 17.5 of the Bible describes a woman astride a seven-headed beast: 'And upon her forehead was a name written, MYSTERY, BABYLON THE GREAT, THE MOTHER OF HARLOTS AND ABOMINATIONS OF THE EARTH.'

Some commentators regard this famous insult as directed towards the established church of Rome, considered corrupt and degenerate as it took on more trappings of the state. This is unconvincing, as the biblical texts were penned in a period that was a melting pot of Semitic religious and philosophical traditions, in the first few centuries of Christianity, before it was made the state religion of the Roman Empire under Emperor Constantine, around 312 CE.

Gordon Rattray Taylor contends that the early Church was concerned with stamping out traces of the old pagan religion (established around women-centred worship), which were incompatible with the emerging ethos of monotheism. In his book *History of Sex* he describes the new religious view as characterized by a repressive attitude to sex, an ascetic fear of pleasure and an emphasis on non-sexual chastity. All women, but especially prostitutes, were seen as sinful and inferior. So the insult might have implicated the goddess cults of the ancients. However, in a world where women had lost respect, having sex with a prostitute – even if she still had some of the glamour of the sacred – was now seen as aligning oneself with the world of the impure, rather than with the world of spirit.

MULIER SUPER BESTIA.

Commentators have described the 'Harlot' as either a corrupt church organization, or as representative of pagan goddess worship.

Shamanism and the natural world

The early great goddesses such as Cybele, Artemis, Diana and Ceres were often seen as a mediating force between nature and the human. This is also seen in Tibetan Buddhism, which retains relics of practice from the earlier Bon religion, which used a shamanic model for integrating the human and natural world. Since Paleolithic times, shamanic techniques (associated particularly with northern cultures such as Siberia, Mongolia and Native Amerindian) included shamans inhabiting animals, or gods in animal forms, in order to enter the supernatural world and there mediate on behalf of humans.

In *The Tree of Life*, Roger Cook describes the travels of the shaman to the sky and the underworld in a bridge formed by the sacred pole in the middle of a yurt. At various steps along his journey, the shaman summons spirits with persistent drumming. According to Cook, his drum is believed to have been carved from a single branch of the great cosmic tree.

Transforming nature

Shamans described shape-shifting, entering other forms in order to travel to parallel worlds to communicate with the spirit world, whether these were totemic or the world of deceased ancestors. Shamanism generally was concerned with gaining all-important control over the natural world, in an attempt to find solutions or control environmental and arbitrary misfortune. On a deeper level, shamanic practices were dedicated to balancing life forces, creating harmony between this world and the other, healing disease and restoring life-giving cycles.

A Mongolian yurt-shaped stone shrine on the grasslands.
Yurts provided a place for shamans to access the spirit world.

Darkness and regeneration

In the days before effective medical treatment and our consummate control of the environment, much effort was expended in early communities on getting the gods to intercede on our behalf, in an attempt to avoid the often arbitrary fates that could befall anyone at any moment. Survival was a daily struggle and infectious disease rife. Until very recently childbirth was extremely dangerous, ending in death for many mothers, and as stillbirths and early child deaths were more common than not; the association between women, sex and death is unsurprising. Among early peoples, the power of regeneration was associated with

This detail from the 21st dynasty Egyptian Book of the Dead *papyrus shows a kneeling figure receiving the eye of Horus: symbol of protection, power and health.*

This carving on rock from predynastic Egypt (c. 4000–3500 BCE) shows the goddess Hathor as a stylized cow's head. The feminine soul of the celestial firmament is depicted as stars.

fertility and women, because of their obvious role in bringing forth life and nurturing offspring. One of the key functions of the goddess, and one of her most mysterious powers, was to transform death into life.

The dark goddess

While the celebration of Inanna was associated with erotic joy and fertile abundance, myths also described her descent to the underworld and battle with dark forces which were necessary to bring life back into balance.

Mystical ideas about death and reincarnation constellated about the goddess and her role in the natural cycle of life; of death and rebirth. Just as the seasonal cycle involves the death of plant life each winter and its regeneration each spring, so the goddess was considered to preside over trips to the underworld in the dark times where she negotiated with or consorted with dark and potent forces, usually to re-emerge into the upper world, transformed and reinvigorated, bringing the benefit to her community.

I am Isis,
I am she who is called goddess by women
I gave and ordained laws for humans
which noone is able to change,
I divided the earth from the heavens
I ordered the course of the sun and the
moon
I appointed to women to bring their
infants to birth in the tenth month
I made the beautiful and the shameful
to be distinguished by nature
I established punishment for those
who practise injustice
I am Queen of rivers and winds
and sea
I am in the rays of the sun
Fate hearkens to me
Hail Egypt that nourishes me.

2nd century CE hymn,
The Many Attributes of Isis quoted in
The Feminine Dimension of the Divine,
Joan C. Engqelsman

Seasonal cycles

The need to influence either the natural world or the divinities related to nature was an established part of religious ritual. Until recent times the importance of propitiating divinities – winning them over to the role of supporting our human needs – often at relevant stages of the seasonal growth of important cereals and other crops, was crucial to the stability of society. This key function has persisted right through to medieval times in the figure of the corn maiden or corn mother.

The corn mother

This figure embodied the fertility of spring throughout peasant Europe. Such motifs common in early goddess worship are still to be found in ancient Greek and Roman mythologies as well as in Old Irish, Welsh, Norse, German, Baltic and Slavic traditions.

Until recently, in rural parts of Germany, the Corn Mother was believed to be present in the last sheaf of corn on the field, which was carried joyfully home and honoured as a divine being. It was placed in the barn, and at threshing time brought out for the corn-spirit to appear once again. In Bruck in Bavaria, the last sheaf was plaited into the shape of a woman by the oldest married woman in the village. The finest ears were plucked and woven into a floral wreath, worn by a village girl in a ritual procession to the barn. In the spring, the grain might be scattered amongst the young corn, calling once again on the fertilizing power of the corn to bless the crop. Ancient Greeks referred to the dead as demeteroi and, in a reference to Demeter as a corn mother, they sowed corn on graves, symbolizing the descent of Demeter's daughter to the land of the dead.

Annual sexual rites

In Europe, May Day is a relic of fertility customs that may have included enactments derived from the ancient sacred marriage, which proved very popular among peasants. Fertility goddesses such as the Hungarian goddess Boldog (possibly related to the Old Sumerian goddess, Bau) were venerated each season. Sex was probably part of this celebration of the life-giving abundance of the goddess, in which sacred sexual rites ensured the success of the crop. The remnants of these widespread and ancient spring rites can be seen even in the persistence of the Celtic festival of Beltane (fire of Bels), a fire festival that celebrated the coming of summer and abundant fertility. It involved singles camping overnight in woodlands, collecting flowers and plants, and spending the night making love around bonfires – resulting in a cluster of marriages.

Sacrifice as sacrament

Fundamental to understanding the deeper significance of such rites is the widespread idea that sexual union was necessary to maintain the world and its abundance. Ritual sex helped to re-create life-giving processes and from the ancient Sumerians to the mysteries of the Greeks, ecstatic Dionysian rites and Celtic celebrants – and multitudes of others – the participants in these rites were all doing their bit to sustain the creative energies of our world. According to anthropologist James Frazer, in some earlier cultures men may have been sacrificed in autumnal rituals of the end of days. The myth of the dying God-king (whether Dumuzi, Adonis, Attis or Osiris) and his ritual sacrifice was documented by Frazer in his

*Revellers at the Beltane fire society's annual festival on Edinburgh's
Calton Hill. The ancient Gaelic festival of Beltane traditionally
marked the beginning of summer.*

1920s compendium on pagan rituals, *The Golden Bough*. The Great
Mother (Inanna, Astarte, Isis, Artemis) remained supreme, while her
consort was sacrificed. The horned one, stag king and even Bonfire Night
are relics of old pagan customs of sacrifice of the consort, invoked in
order to cede power to the cycle of feminine renewal after the darkness
of the winter. At certain periods priests and rulers accrued their divine
legitimacy through consorting with priestesses and goddesses. Making
love could represent both sacrifice and sacrament – although some
consorts were replaced after a year.

Sex and death

In the central Mediterranean, hundreds of womb-shaped tombs dating from the late fifth millennium BCE have been found. The symbolism associated with such burials included triangles, snake coils, spirals, concentric circles and the use of red ochre, and prominent vulvas: as we shall see in the chapter on Tantra (page 222), such images abound to this day in India. Gimbutas associated these graves with uterine symbolism in which the tomb is seen to function symbolically as a conduit (womb) for rebirth. In Eastern religions, the relationship between sex, death and transformation developed in a different way to that of the West. Here, death often symbolizes the death of the self – the ego – as well as our identification with the material world.

The little death of orgasm can be related to the much larger loss of self that is pursued in sacred sex rituals. The Tibetans are aware that the search for self-awareness can lead to the utter extinction of reality as we know it and, as a memento mori, celebrate this by drinking ceremonial wine from a skull. Certain Hindu Tantrics of the 'left-hand path' – so called because they outrageously flout religious conventions – congregate in cremation grounds for ritual practices, which include alcohol and sex.

The books of the dead

The Tibetans and Egyptians penned many books of the dead, the former providing instructions for avoiding the endless cycle of births and deaths (re-incarnations) that they believed occurred until one was sufficiently evolved to become enlightened, the latter providing detailed instructions

Papyrus depiction of the mummified god laid out on a slab with the serpent and his life-giving erect phallus.

for the journey through the underworld. If sex was seen as a doorway to the surrender of the ego among Tibetan Buddhists, then death is the final surrender. In *The Tibetan Book of Living and Dying*, published in 1992, Sogyal Rinpoche, a teacher in the Dzogchen tradition, described the techniques involved in assuring one's liberation at the moment of death, a key goal of spiritual practice.

The goddess and the underworld

Sex and death may have been at the heart of ancient Greek mysteries involving the goddess Demeter and her daughter Persephone, who was kidnapped by the king of the underworld so that he could marry her. The consummation of their sexual relationship resulted in the death of living things on earth. Once reunited with her grieving mother, new plant life burst forth in abundance. Demeter was sometimes described as a corn goddess and, in mythology, Demeter's abandonment of the world during her grief-stricken search for her abducted daughter in the depths of the underworld was the explanation for winter's famine. It was the fruits of sexual knowledge that ultimately bound Persephone to hell for half the year, symbolized by her eating the seeds of pomegranate offered her by the lord of the underworld. During this half of the year the earth was in famine, while for the other half of the year that she was reunited with her mother, the world once again rejoiced with its profusion of bounty: grains, fruits and flowers.

The Greek poet Hesiod (c. 700 BCE) described how, in the early creation myth, Eros sprang forth from the primordial chaos, with the Earth (Gaia) and the underworld. This is the creation myth that underpins many of the ceremonies or 'mysteries' of Greek life.

The Eleusinian mysteries

The ceremonies at Eleusis, the most important religious centre in ancient Greece, were performed in the name of Demeter and Persephone and are thought to have involved fasting, feasting and sacrifice, and to have centred on secret initiations. Enacted over a couple of millennia, and showing many similarities with the Near Eastern and Egyptian mysteries mentioned above, they probably involved entering the world of the divine in some kind of altered state of consciousness. Intoxicating substances may have been used, equally trance and incubation practices were well established. According to Plato (429–347 BCE), 'the ultimate design of the Mysteries ... was to lead us back to the principles from which we descended ... a perfect enjoyment of intellectual [spiritual] good.'

4th-century BCE terracotta votive tablet, depicting initiation celebrations associated with the Eleusinian mysteries.

Mother, son, brother, sister

Early myths elaborated the relationship between mother and daughter, goddess and consort, and then possibly mother and son. An example is the 4th-century Guhyasamaja Buddhist Tantra of Secret Assembly, which refers to ritual union between siblings, and between mother and son.

The myths about mother and son copy earlier myths about the goddess and her consort. The earlier figure of the lover evolves into the son and in some periods like ancient Egypt, son and lover are merged.

In pre-dynastic Egypt, the myth of the goddess and her son-lover was not seen as incestuous but as part of the organizing principle of Eros, with the ritual marriage oof a goddess and her mortal son symbolizing the relationship between the fertile mother/earth and human culture. This pair probably started as a triad – of divine mother, her consort and their child (originally a daughter).

Among dynastic Egyptians the succession of the pharaoh was therefore matrilineal and, as the earlier myths ordained, the power of the pharaoh was conferred by his relationship with his wife, who was ideally his sister. The holy of holies – the rite that imbued him with power – was a sacred sexual rite; without which his power was latent or symbolic. Even throughout the transition to a kingship system of organization, in

This bronze statue shows Isis nursing Horus in her form as the cow goddess Hathor.

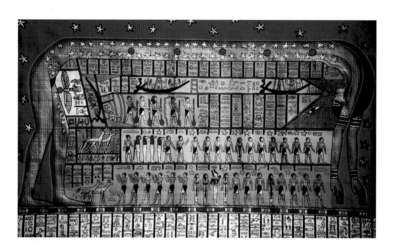

Nut, the sky goddess, stretches over the pharaohs in the Valley of the Kings in infinite embrace with Geb, earth god, begetting siblings who will later unite in sexual rites.

ancient Egypt pharaohs were expected to marry their sisters in order to gain access to some of the power invested in these sacred women. Where they didn't actually marry their own sister they were expected to do so symbolically, and in later times the high priestess stood in for the sanctifying role of the goddess.

There is also evidence pointing towards esoteric sexual rites as a sacrament with the high priestess, specifically in order to legitimate the pharaoh's right to rule. Later invaders of Egypt, both Arab and Christian, hacked off the statuary depictions of erections – either hidden depictions of the pharaoh, or the numerous erections of the god Min – in temples throughout Egypt. During the festival of The Coming Forth of Min, his role in assuring fertility (of grain) was honoured with orgiastic celebration and the consumption of lettuce (which emitted a milky sap – like semen). The temple of the neighbouring goddess Hathor, in Denderra, was inundated with offerings of wooden phalluses, and rituals involved the god and goddess.

Sacred mother

We know from later civilizations such as that of the Greeks that it was believed that statues could be animated by divine presence. We know from ithyphallic carvings in ancient Egyptian temples that sacred marriage was likely an esoteric religious practice – whether it was carried out by a priestess and pharaoh, or symbolically through statues or other intermediaries.

In the creation myths of the ancient Egyptians, the sky goddess Nut made love with the earth and so begat Isis and Osiris. You can see Nut's form painted in the star-spangled lapis lazuli blue that adorns the roofs of the temples of the pharaohs in the Valley of the Kings. The incestuous relationship between Isis and her brother Osiris provided a template for the intermarriage of siblings preferred by rulers. Isis (her name a variant of star) partnered her brother Osiris, and after his dismemberment in battle, Isis searched for the pieces in order to reassemble his body – including his most precious member – and make love. This miraculous resurrection resulted in their child Horus being born after his father's death.

The image of Isis nursing her son was worshipped into the 6th century CE, prefiguring the image of the Virgin and baby Jesus that is venerated throughout Catholic countries to this day. From the time of ancient Greece and Rome, the motifs of the sacred relationship between mother and son, and the precious child begat from union with the divine, persisted – although with genders later realigned according to the rise of patriarchal culture. The same elements are found in some depictions of the Virgin Mother and her grown son the Christ, for whom the Mater Dolorosa weeps tears as he suffers on the cross. Her tears are reminiscent of earlier figures who wept over the loss of their lover/sons.

Virgin cult

Although the Virgin Mary's perfection was presented as being partly due to her freedom from the stain of original sin via the immaculate conception, from 431 CE her cult as the mother of Christ was accepted by the Church and the image of mother and child venerated. Having known such suffering herself, when her son was nailed to the cross, she was widely venerated as the mediator between suffering mankind and Christ. The Virgin was variously worshipped as the bride of Christ, the personification of the Church, or the queen of Heaven – and adored with epithets once taken from older goddess cults. Attributes of compassion, kindness and wisdom were naturally accorded her.

Hellenistic statue of Isis Fortuna retains Hathor's horns and crescent moon.

Sexuality and status

Among the classical Greeks the relationships of established citizens with their young male lovers had more social status than the relationships these same citizens had with their wives. Like slaves and foreigners, women had no votes in the emerging democracy of Athens, and were expected to keep to their domestic arena, the limited one of children and hearth. Women who chose not to marry had a limited number of ways of creating an independent life. Of the very few options available, occasionally prostitution could bring wealth, status and independence, as we see from the inscription of a woman called Rhodopis, who dedicated offerings to a temple in her name at Delphi. Plato's *Symposium* extolled the power of Eros and the homo-erotic pleasures of love. Women could also take female lovers. There is little information on lesbian practices stretching back to pre-history. The poet Sappho, who lived from the 7th century BCE on the island of Lesbos, penned erotic lines that celebrated women. Although her name has been claimed by sapphists and lesbians, we don't know the details of her personal sexual life and how she might have viewed her relationships with women.

The institution of marriage

Right up to the christianizing of the Roman Empire, a wide diversity of customs concerning sex and relationships was common. Homosexual experience, particularly for men, was widely accepted, as was a range of practices including polygamy, prostitution, the sexual use of slaves and even bestiality. Marriage, whether monogamous or polygamous, was

This detail of a late 19th century painting by F.A. Bridgeman shows a
romanticized portrait of Sappho, Greek goddess and poet.

Demon pushing the damned into the mouth of 'leviathan' – a sea serpent – in this 12th century church carving in Aveyron, France.

regarded as an institution primarily for purpose of reproduction, with marriages arranged by family and the community.

Divorce was common and relatively easy – for men. All of this was to change with the Christian message of chastity – whether this referred to a celibate lifestyle that left one free to concentrate on matters of the spirit or to the ideal of a conjugal relationship that mirrored the relationship between man and God. Following the statement attributed to Jesus, 'What God has joined together, let no one put asunder ...' the Catholic church made divorce inadmissable.

Sex and sin

The Church was to become more repressive as it became more established. Scholar Elaine Pagels argues that St Augustine's notion of original sin was completely antithetical to the prevailing sexual mores of the time. In her view, the acceptance of this doctrine by the Church has irreversibly corrupted our experience of sexuality, and barred us from genuine moral and political freedom right through to the present.

Throughout the Middle Ages sodomy was considered sinful – and even punishable by death. However, where individuals could escape the controlling grasp of the Church and its edicts, individuals could and did choose unconventional lifestyles.

Prior to the Victorian era, gender seemed of more practical relevance to the lifestyle choices homosexuals made than did sexuality. Some women chose to live as men in order to gain the privileges associated with masculinity in a world where women had very few rights. In a number of cultures across the world, some men have lived as women, and in some cases had husbands.

The classical Greeks

In the classical and ancient world, the human body was considered a microcosm of the macrocosm, or universe, in which the individual was related to spirits, ancestors, gods and demons, heavenly beings and heavenly bodies (stars and planets). Not only did the laws of the natural world directly influence the life of an individual, but what went on inside the individual could affect these complex inter-relationships. This is the kind of thinking that underlies astrology.

We now call this style of thinking magical – in the sense that acting on one thing was thought to affect another realm – and supernatural, in the sense of being acted on by divine beings (or also, witches and sorcerers). The concept of the evil eye was a widespread explanation for misfortune right up to the advent of modern medicine, assuming a causal connection between the ill will of others and personal misfortune.

I visited the site of an incubation chamber – once a healing temple near Ephesus in present-day Turkey – where the sick would sleep in order to receive a direct message via a dream sent from the god associated with healing, Asclepius. In the temple complex the patients' dreams were once interpreted as a guide indicating therapeutic interventions such as divination, incubation or herbs. Patients prepared as for a temple visit by fasting, bathing, praying and making a sacrifice. For the ancient Greeks, philosophy was about love of wisdom, not empty

This fresco from Pompeii depicts the winged god Mercury holding a caduceus. Asclepius, the son of Apollo and god of healing, was represented by a snake wound around a staff representing the Tree of Life.

rhetoric, and to access it one had to go back to basics – back to the existential ground of one's own being. Philosophers used the priestly rituals provided by their religious affiliations. By the time of the Renaissance, in the late Middle Ages, natural philosophy, which sought to understand and refine the laws of nature such as the movement of the planetary bodies and the mechanisms of health and disease, gradually replaced supernatural explanations for natural events and phenomena.

The elements of life

An example of this change in thinking is the way in which, from the time of Hippocrates in the 5th century BCE, health and personality were thought to be composed of individual admixtures of the four humours –

the four elements that made up all of life in various combinations. Health was a matter of balance both within the body and between man and his world. Aristotle taught that all matter – from wood, to rocks, to plants and human beings – was composed of four irreducible elements: water, earth, fire and air. The proportion of each element was what determined its

The four elements thought to compose the universe: Earth, Fire, Water and Earth.

Plato's Beautiful Love

The writings of Plato (429–347 BCE) have hugely influenced philosophy to this day. However, it is important to remember that the context of philosophy in ancient Greece involved knowledge gained through shamanic ritual, trance and healing rites as well as analytic thought, and that such knowledge was valued and disseminated through teaching and initiation, within a closed group.

Plato discoursed on the notion of all matter as being the external expression of a contemplative deity – the One – an idea common to later mystery traditions and he held that the world as we know it is a distortion of the world of perfect forms, or eternal ideas such as goodness, beauty and justice. These ideal forms provide the template for the things we perceive to be real and true. Man should recognize what we see is not necessarily real, the soul exists in harmony with these forms, and he should explore the realm of the good.

Plato saw love as motivated by a longing for the highest form of beauty – The Beautiful – and as the power that motivates us to reach the sublime. For Plato, Eros motivated the drive for greater and greater unions. According to his follower Plotinus, the 3rd-century founder of Neoplatonism, love was balanced with concern for the lover (*agape*). This vision of a multi-dimensional cosmos infused with love became a theme of neo-Platonic schools. Plotinus revived Platonic philosophy incorporating Gnostic thinking (derived from first-hand mystical experience).

final form. Aristotle's natural philosophy heralded the separation between body and soul, which led to the division between man and the divine. This split later became entrenched in our Western world view as Cartesian duality – we think about everything in terms of opposites and polarity rather than harmony and complements, and our current concern with re-uniting these opposites can be seen as a search for a lost sense of wholeness. The links between the individual and the cosmos have undergone centuries of change and separation since the Greeks. Yet the Greek philosophers were firmly embedded within traditions that valued mystical knowledge and many were actively involved in mystery cults. The pursuit of this knowledge involved long-standing practices of initiation and incubation, in which seekers communed with other worlds. A student of Pythagoras called

For Persephone, induction into carnal knowledge involved death, but a death that contained the seeds of rebirth or transformation.

Parmenides (5th century BCE) is commonly credited as the founder of western rationalism. Parmenides was a healer and priest of Apollo who guided initiates into rites of incubation and the stillness of death where they, like he, might receive the words of Persephone, goddess of the underworld.

His famous poem, only fragments of which survive, describes a journey to the palace of a goddess who welcomes Parmenides and instructs him in the two ways – that of Truth and the deceptive way of Belief, 'which is no truth at all'; but an illusion.

'Young man in the company of immortal charioteers
And mares which carry you, arriving at our house,
Welcome, since in no way a bad fate has sent you forth to go
On this road – for truly it is far from the beaten path of humans –
But rather Right) and Justice. You must hearken to learn everything,
Both the unshaking heart of well-rounded Truth. And the opinions of
mortals, in which there is no true assurance. But nevertheless you
shall learn these things also, how the things that seem
Must really be accepted to be continuously pervading everything ...'

Translation by Professor Cherubin, 2005

For scholar Peter Kingsley the poem is not an allegory (or a meta-physical exploration), but an account of an actual meeting with the goddess in the incubation chambers of a temple. The purpose of this journey 'down to the world of death while still alive' was to transform personal consciousness. Such journeys are key to traditions both East and West, part of our common ancestry.

The Delphic oracle

For centuries before the spectacular rise of Delphi as the centre of divination in the classical world, Greeks used caves such as the huge Corycian one near Delphi, named after a nymph, as a temenos, or sacred space, in which to commune with nymphs, satyrs, and goddesses and gods, and to leave offerings. The Corycian Cave was a place of worship for local people, whereas the Delphic Oracle was dedicated to Apollo and became a major site of pilgrimage from the 11th century BCE. However, the traditions of wise women and seers have ancient precedent even well before the Delphic oracle, the Sibyls and other prophetesses of the period. 'Delphi' comes from the root for womb and was dedicated to the earth goddess Gaia, probably as far back as Neolithic times, until Apollo slew the python guarding the sanctuary (the offspring of Gaia).

This wood engraving of 1890 shows the prophecies of the oracle of Delphi at the Temple of Apollo, home of the famous dictum 'Know Thyself'.

The famed oracle was actually the priestess of the shrine, and could only be consulted for nine days a year, according to the writings of the priest, Plutarch. Supplicants and rulers came from various Greek states, and further afield, to seek advice. Above the doors of the temple of Apollo was the inscription, 'Know Thyself'. The priestess delivered her messages while in a trance state from her position over a cleft in the rock thought to harbour a serpent; contemporary geologists prefer to credit ethylene fumes. Her messages were famed for their ambiguity: one had to know oneself in order to interpret them correctly, and to reflect on their message before taking action.

The Plataean Tripod, dedicated to Apollo, which was moved from Delphi to Constantinople marking the site of the new Omphalos. Three snakes coiled around each other to create a tall pillar.

The voice of the oracle was only silenced once ancient Greek civilization was eclipsed by the rise of the Roman Empire, and in particular by the ascendency of the Christian religion. Around 360 CE the last pagan emperor sent a message to the oracle from Constantinople, receiving the reply that her voice was now quenched and that civilization had fallen. Whereas Delphi had once been considered the navel, or omphalos, of the world, it was superceded by the church of Hagia Sophia – the Holy Wisdom (see page 92) – in Constantinople, which became the religious centre of the Eastern Orthodox Church for the next thousand years.

Hermetic beliefs

In the first century CE Alexandria, on the Mediterranean coast of Egypt, with its famed library, was a hothouse of philosophical enquiry, where the works of the ancient Greeks, Romans, Egyptians and Jews were mined to produce new works of alchemy, and cabbalistic and magical speculation. Intellectuals inspired by the Hellenistic Egyptian writings attributed to a mythological figure called Hermes Trismegistus flourished in Alexandria, and became known as Hermetics.

These Hermetic groups traced their philosophical heritage to the Greeks. Many seemed broadly concerned with investigating how to purify the human realm of demonic forces and regain our divine nature. According to Hermetic theology, humans rank higher than angelic beings, because of our innate capacity to unite with the spiritual realm and to marry higher and lower worlds. Hermetic beliefs subsequently heavily influenced the Western esoteric tradition, which spawned a host of groups such as the Rosicrucians in the 15th century and the Golden Dawn at the turn of the 19th century.

The Rosicrucian symbol of the Hermetic order of the Golden Dawn.

An architectural detail of a column in Modena, Italy, features a hermaphrodite, which transcends gender.

The hermaphrodite

The androgynous divine figure, half man, half woman, is found in sites from ancient Indian temple sculptures to classical Greece. An amalgamation of the principles of Eros and Logos, or heart and mind, the hermaphrodite blends Aphrodite, the goddess of love, with Hermes, messenger of the gods.

In early cultures, and some in the Far East, the hermaphrodite symbolized the ability of the world to consume itself and be reborn. For the Hermetics, the hermaphrodite was a potent symbol of the integration of the instinctual world with that of reason; the revealed manifest world of phenomena and the spirit world of the divine. Hermaphroditus, the bisexual son of Aphrodite and Hermes, had both male and female sexual characteristics. All three gods were characterized as erotic and sexual.

Alchemy

Alchemy (from the Arabic 'al-chimia') was an esoteric discipline that blended Egyptian and later Islamic mystical thought with Greek and Latin philosophy to create a new type of philosopher who worked through enquiry and experimentation, prefiguring the science of chemistry.

Its methodology used the chemical processes of distillation and sublimation in order to remove the superfluous and leave the pure – the 'quintessence', considered a spiritual rather than a material quality. The active principle was fire, so heat might be applied to encourage the physical processes of transmutation.

The alchemical transformation of base metals into gold, and the search for spiritual gold were both real and philosophical, and conceptualized as the search for the philosopher's stone.

The learned Nestorian sect split from the Church after suggesting that the divine aspects of Jesus and his mother were separable from the human aspects. They were subsequently expelled from Constantinople in 431 as heretics. Their works were later developed and refined by Arab scholars who were heavily involved in alchemical experimentation, from whence they were reintroduced to Europe after the Dark Ages, once Catholicism released its tyrannical grip on control of heresy.

Alchemy peaked in the medieval period and persisted into the 18th century. It concerned ideas about the construction of the world that have only relatively recently been replaced with a scientific understanding. This development has helped strip away notions of the spiritual basis for matter, and contributed to a materialist approach to science.

This 1519 illustration shows alchemists processing the raw material of life to isolate the quintessence, or the 'fifth element'.

At the time the world was believed to be composed of four elements (water, earth, fire and air) in various combinations, (see page 54) rather than the elements we are familiar with today from the periodic table.

The combination and proportion of each element determined the final form of every kind of matter. Alchemists endlessly experimented in order to transform matter, using techniques of heating, drying and moistening, in accordance with the humoral thinking that predominated until the advent of the recent scientific era ushered in a whole new paradigm. The understanding that there was a limited amount of matter in the universe blew certain notions of alchemy apart.

The chymical wedding

Whereas mainstream thinking was influenced by the split between mind and matter, alchemy held that matter and spiritual essence were two different forms of the same fundamental principle. One consequence of this belief was that you could influence the spirit realm by working on matter. Drawing on a familiar metaphor for the unification of different materials, the transformation of matter into spirit through the unification of opposites was called the chymical wedding. The chymical wedding referred to the conjunction of gold (Sol) and silver (Luna) and was compared to the 'sacred marriage' of body and spirit. The offspring of the union was the philosopher's daughter, or the philosopher's stone (lapis).

The Sol and Luna poem was famously illustrated in the 1550 *De Alchimia Opuscula*, and known as the *Rosarium Philosophorum* ('The Rosary of the Philosophers').

This miniature from the German alchemical text 'Splendour soils', depicts the forces of the sun and moon.

O Luna, surrounded by me
and sweet one mine
you become fine and powerful as I am
O Sol you are recognisable over all others
you need me as the cock needs the hens.

Here king and queen lie dead
the soul departs in great haste
here the 4 elements separate
and from the body the soul departs
... here the soul comes from the sky, fine and clear
and resurrects the philosopher's daughter.

From *Alchemy*
***and Mysticism* by Alexander Roob**

In the first phase of the Rosarium Philosophorum, the soul rises from the body to be unified with the spirit in Heaven. Later it would descend to be reunited with the body through mysterious alchemical processes.

Sex as metaphor

The Rosarium series of woodcut images depict the sexual union of the king and the queen, in the Fountain of Mercury, as a metaphor for the alchemical process. Sexual union unites the opposing principles of matter and spirit, in the form of a hermaphrodite. Sexual union was depicted as a means of co-creating the world in the image of the divine. Alchemists used these terms to describe the complex relationships between reality, matter and spirit.

Alchemy and Jung

According to the contemporary Jungian interpretation of the language of mystical union, Sol and Luna symbolize consciousness and the unconscious, and in the alchemical world view the conjunction of the two produced the element mercury, associated with communication. Here mercury is the primal material that needs to be imbued with the power alchemically generated through the sacred union.

Like the Christian Gnostics before them, the alchemists were concerned with the perfectibility of man, and the primary mechanism for this seemed to be through the unification of opposites – harking back to an earlier vision of natural life as integrated and holistic. One aim of the alchemists was to bring base matter – symbolizing God's imperfect creation – back to a state of perfection.

For psychoanalyst Carl Jung the path of personal growth involved maturing psychologically, and developing the 'Self' or personal soul that connects each of us to the universe (the symbol of the Self is the circle, or mandala, which represents completion). Dreams or trance states contain a message from the Self that can be used for growth. Jungian analysts see man's perfectibility as a personal concern and the primary goal of psychic growth.

However, an alchemical perspective on wholeness and healing necessitates entering into relationship with the other, through the Gnostic imagination. It's a world of direct experience, and active imagination is a great tool – it's not just a matter of theory and philosophy. Active imagination is the modern technique that achieves the same purpose as

Jung explored his own unconscious through dreams,
reflections and drawing mandaals (circles) for several years
afterbreaking with Freud in 1913, over Freud's theory of
(infantile) sexuality.

incubation – a means to meet spiritual beings and experience revelation. Psychoidal alchemist Jeffrey Raff extends Jung's thought into the Gnostic dimension, suggesting that it is through the seeker's wedding with Sophia as a spiritual being that we make an individual relationship with the mysterious, ineffable divine. Such a meeting is so profound, that the

Jung believed that the inner world could offer guides and mentors
that were rooted in ancient myths – part of our collective
unconscious.

language of love is used to describe the personal transformation that
can result. In the 14th-century alchemical text *Aurora consurgens*
('Rising dawn'), the anonymous author – possibly the saint, Thomas
Aquinas – describes the mystical marriage of Sophia with the Divine,
through the male part of himself. By allying himself to a sacred being,
allowing her to become his guide, man's own nature becomes more divine.
Man can enter a loving relationship that creates a numinous sense of Self.
Raff quotes Sophia's revelation to Thomas:

'I am the flower of the field and the lily of the valleys;
I am the mother of fair love and of fear' and of knowledge
and of holy hope.
As the fruitful vine I have brought forth a pleasant odour and my
flowers are the fruit of honour and riches. I am the bed of my beloved,
which three score of the most valiant ones surrounded, all holding
swords upon their thigh because of fears in the night. I am all fair
and there is no spot in me; looking though the windows, looking
through the lattices of my beloved, wounding his heart with one
of my eyes and with hair of my neck.
I am the sweet smell of ointments, giving an odour
above all aromatical spices ...
I am the most prudent virgin, coming forth as the Dawn,
sing exceedingly, elect as the sun, fair as the moon, besides
what is hid within.'

Sophia was considered by the Gnostics to be the personification of divine knowing. For Raff, Sophia may be an insubstantial principle, but she is not a dream – just as Kingsley describes Parmenides' meeting with the goddess Persephone as real. For these two Gnostic scholars, the goddess is an ally who needs contact with the realm of humans in order to manifest her wisdom in the world. Goddesses of old were believed to manifest through emanations, a sort of passive process of diffusion.

The Gnostic seeker provides a conduit for her to manifest her qualities, through their relationship. This appears to be the deeper esoteric understanding of the sacred marriage, or hieros gamos, in which this ritual manifests healing cosmic energies.

A modern interpretation of the alchemy of relationship

Applying an alchemical understanding of the sacred marriage to contemporary romantic relationships allows us to see a love relationship as a transformative process, in which inner awareness can call into being the power of the sacred principle. In *The Crucible of Love*, psychotherapist Jay Ramsay defines 'alchemical' stages in an 'erotic soul relationship'. After 'coniunctio', where two people come together, they enter a period of love and relative harmony, during which each presents their best sides to one another.

The couple inevitably enter the 'nigredo', or dark phase, in which each partner tries to change the other. In a strong relationship, they begin to feel safe enough to express disappointments, grief and trauma from the past. This stage requires the breaking down of two separate egos in order for the real work of relating to begin. In the purifying phase of 'solutio', as personal egotism subsides the deeper essence of each partner can manifest, and the alchemy process begins to work at a fundamental level. Once each partner learns to listen to the other, they can drop expectations and judgements. Each individual learns how to be themselves in the relationship, while also committing to being together. According to Jungian theory, this stage also involves a woman integrating her inner masculine and a man integrating his inner feminine to create an inner marriage of masculine and feminine elements. This is the stage of the union of opposites (see Jung on animus and anima, page 146).

A contemporary reinterpretation of coniunctio uses it as a metaphor to describe a partnered relationship that functions like a crucible. Sexual energies, representing masculine and feminine, can be transformed just as base metals were believed to turn to gold.

The final stage is 'rubedo', red, where two people can now be independent, while appreciating their togetherness, in a union that is greater than the combination of the two individuals.

The energy of the spiritual dimension has now entered the relationship and resurrected the couple. With a shared vision, the couple can now direct their energies outwards, in response to their increased awareness of their fundamental connection with the wider world.

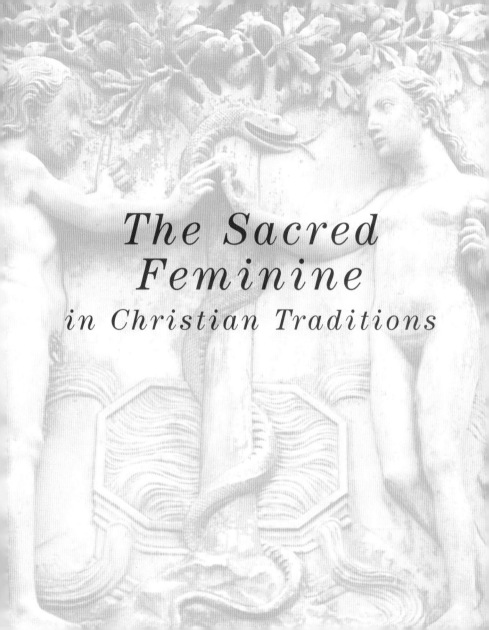

The Sacred Feminine
in Christian Traditions

Gnosticism

The feminine face of God has been central to Gnostic teachings from the time of early Christianity – and one of the reasons why these teachings soon had to be kept private and hidden from the mainstream Church. For instance, the feminine principle of Sophia (wisdom), venerated since the time of the Greeks, was central to Gnostic understandings of the biblical creation myth. Even the word Gnostic comes from the Greek for knowing, and favoured a personal relationship with God, rather than following the rules and rituals of the Church. To the Church, such ideas smacked of paganism, even if Greek civilization provides the moral and intellectual basis of much of Judeo-Christian culture – and it wasn't long before such groups were branded heretical. Christian Gnostic groups pursued their own interpretations of oral and textual traditions, in secret. The Bible and its creation myths were read by groups such as the Valentinians, who flourished from the 2nd to the 4th centuries CE, as spiritual allegories whose messages could be accessed

The divine spark was embodied in Sophia, the goddess of wisdom, here in a temple niche at Ephesus.

Valentinianism

Valentinianism was one of the major Gnostic movements. Founded by Valentinus in the 2nd century CE, it spread throughout the Christian world and lasted for about 200 years, despite attack from more conventional religious figures such as the bishop Tertullian (b. 169 CE).

Valentinus elaborated a complex system, heavily influenced by Platonic philosophy. He described an ideal world (the pleroma) and a lower world of phenomena (the kenoma), both created through the emanations of a formless primal being. The first living beings were thought to have formed in sexually complementary pairs (aeons). Like most Gnostics, the Valentinians believed man is fundamentally flawed, and that he needs to free himself from the material realm to enter the fullness of the pleroma and regain his spiritual or angelic nature.

through an imaginative exploration of symbols and meanings. In 1945 the discovery at Nag Hammadi, in Upper Egypt, of more than 50 original texts used by Gnostic groups threw light on various mystical strands within very early Christianity. Some texts were attributed to women, and many discussed Sophia (wisdom) as part of the creation, alongside God the Father, or else saw her role as one of the aeons and therefore debased.

Illustration of the Ptolomaic system showing
Earth at the centre of the cosmos circled by the seven planets then
known. An early scientific, gnostic interpretation of Bible myths.

Fragment of the Gospel of Thomas, found at Nag Hammadi.

Here the Gnostics saw themselves as an important ally with the divine in redeeming Sophia and helping her to reclaim her power.

Gnostic reinterpretations of biblical texts acknowledged the special relationship between Jesus and Mary Magdalene. Some regarded God as Father and Mother, composed of both masculine and feminine attributes. The Gnostic Theodotus (c. 160 CE), for instance, explained that 'the male and female elements together constitute the finest production of the Mother, Wisdom.' Others cast Adam as immortal and whole – literally one with Eve – before his fateful separation from her, describing Adam as responsible for man's expulsion from paradise by refusing to engage in sacred (sexual) union with Eve. Refusing the sacred aspect of marriage was seen as denying the goddess (as incarnated in women) the recognition she was due.

The texts included apocryphal (alternative) Gnostic versions of biblical myths of creation and salvation; commentaries on themes such as the nature of reality, the soul and how the personal soul relates to the world soul; initiatory texts, (such as *A Valentinian Exposition*); writings dealing with the feminine principle, often called the Divine Sophia; and writings about the lives of Jesus and the apostles, providing a multilayered understanding of the Gnostic world view. Like all esoteric traditions, Gnostic creation myths could be read in a number of ways – and there is still huge debate about the extent to which such readings can be interpreted literally or symbolically.

A fragment from a text entitled *Primal Thought* celebrates the feminine powers of thought, intelligence and foresight, which together made up the ground of a human being. The ground of being is a concept used to express the fundamental nature of existence and is another way of describing God or the Goddess.

I am Thought that dwells in the Light...
She who exists before the All...
I move in every creature...
I am the Invisible One within the All.

I am perception and knowledge,
uttering a Voice by means of Thought.
I am the real Voice.
I cry out in everyone,
and they know that a seed dwells within.

Gnostikos was the term used among Greeks for 'leading to knowledge', and was considered just one form of the

many different kinds of knowledge elaborated by ancient Greek philosophers. Gnostic knowledge involved learning from experience, and was an established method of engagement in spiritual enquiry from at least the time of Plato. Broadly, mysticism expressed the desire for communion with God through personal experience or knowledge. Pagan practices of fasting, incubation and trance gradually metamorphosed into the Christian practices of prayer, contemplation and reflection that we're familiar with today. All these techniques were concerned with developing direct knowledge through the cultivation of states receptive to the grace of God/dess. Among seekers, spiritual longing was seen as a sign of the loss of connection that man once enjoyed with the divine, and the goal of the mystics was to recover a sense of union with the divine. While many contemporary mystics describe God as love, the early Christian Gnostics who talked about the feminine principle of loving wisdom (Sophia) as the true grounding of spirituality were drummed out of the Church and later persecuted as heretics. The existence of these original Gnostic texts indicates that the world of the early Christians was much more diverse than we might imagine from its later history. Also, that by tracing Christian practices we can learn much about the Pagan behaviours before them.

The sacrament of the bridal chamber

Gnostic and Hermetic (see page 60) schools developed complex and sophisticated maps of the universe as a macrocosm whose laws were reflected in the microcosm of the human realm. Due to this close relationship, human actions could impact on the macrocosm. The tradition relevant to the themes in this book is a mystery mentioned in the Bible, called the sacrament of the bridal chamber.

According to a Gnostic reading of 1 Corinthians:

Prepare yourself as a bride expecting her husband, that you may be what I am and I what you are; place the seed of light in your marriage chamber; receive from me your husband, and be received by him.

In certain Gnostic groups sexual union was not regarded as tainted by sin, as it was later, in Christianity. If conducted with the right intention and focus, it could be used as a force for union with the spiritual realm. Valentinians believed that a Gnostic could enter the fullness of the pleroma (or ideal world) in his lifetime, and be permanently joined with the bridegroom (the spiritual plane of existence) in the harmony of oneness. The sacrament of the bridal chamber was one ritual aimed at achieving this mystical union.

A number of texts found at Nag Hammadi refer to sacred love-making. It is not clear whether the sacrament of the bridal chamber involved

William Blake's illumination of Adam and Eve's fall shows the spirit of their union above, evocative of the sacred marriage.

sacred sex rites, although there is no real reason not to suppose such rites weren't practised. Most of our information is gleaned from denunciations; for instance, in his *Adversus Haereses* or 'Against Heresies' (c. 180), Bishop Iraneus in Gaul denounced the mystic Marcus, who led a Christian cult (Marcosians) active in Lyons from around 200 CE in which women acted as prophetesses and ritual sex was practised and

*Late 17th-century miniature shows the alchemical union of king
and queen, sun and moon. The dragon symbolizes volatility.*

called a 'spiritual marriage'. Among Gnostic writings, the sacred marriage symbolized the union of the two aspects of divinity (the individual soul and the divine), in which the awakened soul was imbued with Christ and the Holy Spirit.

The sacred marriage was used as an image of union between the soul and the divine, after which the material world dissolved away to be replaced by the world as the eternal realm. While many scholars assume such writings to be purely symbolic, the similarity to other mysteries involving sacred sex is striking. According to the Gnostic Gospel of Philip, found at Nag Hammadi:

If the woman had not separated from the man, she would not die with the man. His separation became the beginning of death. Because of this, Christ came, in order that he might remove the separation, and again unite the two .... But the woman is united with her husband in the bridal chamber. Those who have been united in the bridal chamber will no longer be separated.

Through union, two lovers could enter into a sacred mystery where their embrace would leave them 'clothed in light'. This interpretation resonates with current knowledge about the power of sacred sex to open us to a reality of a much profounder unity normally associated with mystical experience.

Although many Gnostics considered themselves beyond social convention as regards sex and marriage, the bridal chamber was a key metaphor referring to the marriage between man and God, and matter and spirit.

Custom of the chaste union

By the beginning of the Christian era, social changes meant that the old forms of marriage, in which women were married off without their consent and young men were preferred as sexual partners (for men following the customs of the Greeks and Romans), were replaced by vows in which the couples pledged themselves to one other in a new spirit of equality. These promises reflected the egalitarian ethos of the early Christians. Paul's statement that, 'In Christ there is neither male nor female' (Galatians 3.18) fostered a new spirit of equality evidenced by the close involvement of women in religious communities during the early years of Christianity.

Desexualizing love

Chastity was becoming a valued concept and chastity within marriage was also becoming an ideal. The notion of chastity and virtue did not have the same connotations we think of today – that is, non-sexual – but referred more to the spiritualizing power of a certain quality of love (agape). Even men and women who were vowed to celibacy experimented with 'spiritual marriage'. A large group of women lived as the beloveds (agapetae) of men living the religious life, in which unconditional, self-sacrificing love became the model for the appropriate way to express the love of Christ. Another group of women called the subintroductae lived with clerics, as householders. It is not known whether chaste relationships were sexual or not, and if so, what forms sexual union might have taken. The widespread custom of living with agapetae suggests it was commonly believed priests could find chastity in a perfect love.

St Mary Magdalene repentant but magnificent in front of an image of Christ on the cross.

Chaste bed

Within early Christianity, chaste union referred to a spiritual relationship, for example, between a priest and his beloved – a woman with whom he might live. These relationships were described as based on spiritual love rather than Eros (intimate love). The relationship between a priest and his beloved was conducted primarily through the paradigm of spiritual love.

According to Gnostic belief, God was conceived of as being merged with his own beloved (usually the feminine principle of wisdom), providing a model for this type of chaste union. In the sacred marriage the lover becomes identified with the God who is merged with his own beloved. Loving God and entering into such a chaste relationship was seen as transformative; it sanctifies the relationship. Bishop Iranaeus (c. 200), in his book *Against Heresies*, railed against the Gnostic Christian 'mystery of conjunction' (sacred marriage) interpreting gnostics' belief as follows: loving and joining with a woman would lead to spiritual knowledge while uniting with a woman in a state of lust would ensure that you could not reach gnosis.

Whoever is in the world and loves a woman so that he is not joined to her is not of the truth and will not proceed to truth, but he who is of the

world and is united with a woman (by desire)
will not proceed to truth.

Church leaders gradually spoke out against the chaste union, and observers did not believe that these chaste relationships were particularly chaste, because of regular scandals. The desert ascetic St Jerome wrote:

I blush to speak of it, it is so shocking; yet though sad, it is true. How comes this plague of the agapetae to be in the church? Whence come these unwedded wives, these novel concubines, these harlots, so I will call them, though they cling to a single partner? One house holds them

14th-century illustration of Mary as Queen of Heaven. She is standing on a crescent moon, referring to chastity.

*and one chamber. They often occupy the same bed, and yet they call us
suspicious if we fancy anything amiss ... Both alike profess to have but
one object, to find spiritual consolation from those not of their kin; but
their real aim is to indulge in sexual intercourse. It is on such that
Solomon in the book of proverbs heaps his scorn. 'Can a man take
fire in his bosom,' he says, 'and his clothes not be burned?*

Less esoteric interpretations of the custom of the chaste bed
conceptualized it as a test of the vows of celibacy. Religious men
described sleeping with lovely virgins as a sign of their commitment
to their faith, and so there was widespread sharing of beds between
supposed celibates. In writing against the widespread practice of 'chaste
union' around 400 CE, Archbishop Chrysostom said:

*The notion that this pleasure and love can be keener than that
afforded by living together in a legal marriage probably astounds you,
[but in the case of a spiritual bride] there is no intercourse which
can restrain and relax the frenzy of nature, nor do labour pains and
childrearing dry up her flesh; to the contrary, these virgins stay in
their prime for a long time, since they remain untouched ... These
women retain their beauty until they are forty ... Thus the men who
live with them are stirred by a double desire; they are not permitted
to satisfy their passion through sexual intercourse, yet the basis
for their desire remains intensely potent for a long time.*

A number of Church councils complained about the large numbers of
unmarried women attached to clerics and dozens of edicts ruled against
this practice, until it was stamped out by around 600–700 CE.

Women's role in the Church

The group gathered around Gnostic teacher Valentinus believed that personal experience was the arbiter of the truth of religious precepts, rather than second-hand testimony or accepted tradition. Members of this circle demonstrated their disregard for formal hierarchies by drawing lots at each meeting to decide who would fulfil the various roles of priest, of reader and that of spiritual instruction. They valued all participants, regardless of social status or gender. This egalitarianism was deeply challenging to the mainstream clerics of the day. The extraordinary openness of the early Church was what one would expect from the long history of women as healers, prophets and teachers. Historians speculate that among the Gnostics, as in the communities in ancient Sumer and old Europe (see pages 20 and 22), women were considered equal to men. However, according to scholar Elaine Pagels, by the year 200 CE there were no further records of any women taking prophetic or priestly roles in orthodox churches.

An altar scene at the Santa Maria Magdalena church, Cala Huela province, Spain shows woman at the centre of early Church life.

*This fresco from the catacombs of Rome places Mary as the central
figure to be adored, with her child and saints.*

God and feminine symbolism: Sophia

The absence of feminine attributes and symbolism for God sets mainstream Judaism, Christianity and Islam apart from the world's older religious traditions, which are full of feminine symbolism. Jewish, Christian and Islamic theologians today assert that God is not to be considered in sexual terms at all – yet the language used in worship and prayer to refer to transcendent states often has a markedly erotic flavour. The rapture of some saints, such as Hildegard of Bingen, has sometimes left women mystics at the mercy of a wrathful ecclesiastic authority. Recent decades have seen an acceptance of the role of mystical reverie in creating a personal relationship with the divine.

St Sophia the Divine Wisdom

The Bible refers to heavenly wisdom (Hagia Sophia) as feminine, but for today's Catholics God is indisputably masculine. For Plato, philosophy referred to the love of wisdom (see also page 55, Plato's Beautiful Love). In Plato's political treatise *The Republic*, leaders of the proposed Utopia were philosopher-kings who loved and honoured the feminine wisdom of Sophia.

Among the ancients, Sophia was regarded as the guiding spirit of human development. Her wisdom was that of the heart which encompassed an intuitive and inclusive knowingness of life, incorporating the earlier consciousness of goddess figures from whom all life was born

This Russian icon from 1618 depicts Sophia the Divine Wisdom, the feminine principle that remained in early Christianity as a direct link to the wisdom of the ancient Greeks.

and to whom all life returned in an endless cycle of renewal. Sophia is perhaps the last of a long line of ancient Near Eastern goddesses. She was the personification of divine knowing. The ancients saw the wisdom goddess as enabling us to understand the world and creation and to live in harmony with it; she was the creator of the world at the same time that she was the whole world and creation, and as the wisdom goddess she linked the creation and our understanding of it with her wish to teach us about the world and our need to learn.

The concept of wisdom integrated intuition with clarity and purpose.
These attributes were later assigned to the separate genders.

This is a description of Wisdom, from the Wisdom of Solomon 7:22–30, possibly written by Philo around 100–50 BCE in Alexandria, Egypt:

For in Her there is a Spirit that is intelligent, holy, unique, manifold, subtle, mobile, clear, unpolluted, distinct, invulnerable, loving the good, keen, irresistible, beneficent, humane, steadfast, sure, free from anxiety, all-powerful, overseeing all and penetrating through all spirits that are intelligent and pure and most subtle.

For Wisdom is more mobile than any motion; because of Her pureness She pervades and penetrates all things. For She is a Breath of the power of God, and a pure emanation of the glory of the Almighty; therefore nothing defiled gains entrance into Her. For She is a reflection of eternal light, a spotless mirror of the working of God, and an image of His goodness.'

In the first few centuries of Christianity, Sophia was venerated as the feminine principle of God, in the triad of Father, Son and Holy Spirit. There was a split between a personal soul and the transpersonal spirit. The idea of the trinity was not new; it harked back to earlier triads of maiden, mother and crone, which reflected lunar and seasonal cycles; and to mother, father and son. With the ascendency of Old Testament patriarchs in the established Church, Sophia lost her role as the consort of God, or His feminine face, to become a fallen figure in need of redemption.

Gnostics wanted to redeem the divine figure of Sophia. They believed that Sophia resides in all of us, as divine spark. Gnostics held that knowledge of one's spiritual essence could liberate us from the imperfections of the created world. With the suppression of Gnosticism in the early history of Christianity, wisdom became increasingly associated with God, and the word of God (Logos), handed down in laws from heaven rather than to be discovered through reflection and communion.

Historian Roy Porter describes how the Christian belief in a soul that transcended the flesh and death was rooted in the very Gnostic thinking that the early Church was so concerned to stamp out, and can be found in the metaphysics of ancient Greek philosophers. Gnostic thinking has infiltrated mainstream Christianity in spite of the later efforts of the Roman Catholics to purge such thinking.

Suppression of goddess worship

While many Gnostic sects regarded the flesh as fundamentally flawed, an indicator of the debased condition of mankind after the fall, perversely the Church set a positive value on the embodied self (the soul who is incarnated in a body) in its central narrative of the crucified Son of God.

However, the female body was devalued. The edicts of Christian Emperor Constantine were stripped of the relics of earlier goddess worship, and the feminine was demoted to the profane realm. The realm of spirit and divinity was firmly that of Logos and God. The Virgin's role became one of Christ-bearer, the holy son immaculately conceived, consigning the once close association of Eros and divinity to history. Jesus's disciple Mary Magdalene was possibly smeared as a prostitute. Some of his followers (notably Simon Magus) formed a close relationship with a prostitute who symbolized the fallen feminine – in which Christianity was to play a redemptive role.

El, the Original Creator-god

El was the chief god at the Canaanite city of Ugarit (in modern-day
Syria), which was established in Neolithic times. El (literally 'The')
was praised as father of men, creator, and creator of the creation, with
his consort Asherah. Their sacred marriage produced a son, Yahweh,
who became the Hebrew God of the Old Testament. Many of the early
male gods who were precursors to Yahweh seem to have their origin
in El. The emerging picture of an omnipotent and in some ways
wrathful God among the Semites was a great break from the past; this
God did not derive power from, or even share it with, any goddess, nor
was he conceived to be a divine husband or lover. The growth of the
three monotheistic religions in the Holy Lands perpetuated a wrathful
figure within Christianity; in particular, hell became a place of
punishment for sins or imperfections.

The fall from grace

Central to the Gnostic conception of creation was the idea that the world had fallen from perfection. While orthodox Christianity was concerned with the notion of original sin and the fall from paradise, Gnostics saw creation as rendered impure by demonic forces; their central concern was to redeem life now rather than in the afterlife.

To the Gnostics the biblical notion of sin could perhaps be translated as 'forgetting' – in this case, forgetting our divine nature. Sin wasn't about disobeying laws, obedience, or submission to the word of God, but about recalling our true essence and the eternal nature of reality.

Sophia became a lost goddess who needed the Gnostics to reconnect her with her original sanctity. In the Gnostic interpretation, Mary Magdalene stood in for the redeemed Sophia by becoming the beloved of Christ. Sophia has persisted in contemporary Gnostic groups, where she represents the necessity

Mary Magdalene and Virgin Mary embracing – from a 12th-century Romanesque altarpiece (Barcelona).

of healing the fallen status of the sacred feminine through reuniting the experience of being in a body with the essential purity of the spirit realm.

In this extract from the Gnostic poem known as *The Thunder; Perfect Mind*, poet Alan Jacobs translates Wisdom's words:

> *I am the first and the last,*
> *I am both respected and ignored.*
> *I am both harlot and holy.*
> *I am wife and virgin.*
> *mother and the daughter ...*
> *I am she whose marriage is auspicious,*
> *but I am husbandless ...*
>
> *I am both godless, and she who*
> *knows god is great*
> *I am the one you've contemplated*
> *and mocked ...*
>
> *I am the one who conceals*
> *And then reveals herself ...*
>
> *Those who are close don't know me.*
> *When you are near, I'm distant*
>
> *On the day you're distant I am close*
> *I am within, in your heart*
> *I am your true nature ...*

The 'fallen' woman

According to the Bible, Eve was created by God as a companion for Adam, and they lived in perfect harmony with their environment until Eve was tempted by the serpent to eat the forbidden fruit of the tree of knowledge. This initiation is described within mainstream Christianity as the fall from paradise, and is often invoked as the reason for women's lowly status. Women and their seductiveness, or 'temptation', have come to be widely glossed as being due to an innate 'original sin'. This is a complete reversal of the long-standing pre-Christian tradition of worshipping the sacred feminine. Worship of the feminine included embracing embodiment – enjoying living in a body and the sensuality of our experience.

An alternative Gnostic version of the Fall describes Adam as the embodiment of spirit (psyche) and Eve as the spiritual principle of pneuma (breath). Adam and Eve were created together in God's image, and this god was both male and female. Apocryphal traditions (outside the accepted canon) suggest multiple readings of the creation myth, in which Eve and the snake were bearers of knowledge. In these versions, Eve was wise rather than seductive, and responsible for awakening Adam from his ignorance of his own divine nature.

As an allegory, the Fall is widely associated with consciousness and the loss of man's ego and resulting death and resurrection. The sin associated with Eve can be described by gnostics as the sin of forgetting one's divine origins and identifying with the kenoma.

Likewise, far from being evil, the serpent has been associated for millennia with wisdom and the trance states used by the ancients to access this wisdom. The serpent opened the pair's eyes to knowledge

Adam and Eve with Lilith as the serpent, from the
Speculum Humanae Salvationis, *1455.*

and the truth of their immortal nature. At the same time, Adam and Eve's initiation into worldly knowledge meant entering both knowledge and suffering together – a fundamental part of the human condition – and consciously shouldering the burdens of life, as well as its joys. Therefore Gnostics saw it as their responsibility to improve the lot of man, while helping him find his way back to paradise.

Lilith, the first Eve

An apocryphal version of the creation myth describes the first woman as Lilith, who was made from dust along with Adam. The root of the name Lilith is connected with layil, Hebrew for 'night', and lil, Sumerian (c. 3000 BCE) for 'wind' or 'breath'.

According to the possibly satirical writings around the 6th century attributed to Ben-Sira, (credited with penning Ecclesiasticus, in the 2nd century, one of the wisdom texts of the Old Testament) Lilith was created as man's equal but left Adam after refusing to subordinate herself sexually (explicitly, refusing to take the missionary position). Eve was then fashioned from Adam's rib as his second wife, while Lilith escaped to the desert where she preferred to live with demons. To this day, protective amulets are worn to protect from the wrath of Lilith, now metamorphosed into an archetypally vengeful fury.

Some scholars identify the origins of Lilith in the ancient Sumerian story of Gilgamesh. Samuel Noah Kramer translated a poem that describes how Inanna Queen of Heaven and Earth, (see page 24) went to harvest wood from a willow tree in her garden, but found a serpent living at its base, a Zu bird raising young in its crown, and that Lilith had made a home in its trunk. Gilgamesh smote the snake, causing the bird to fly away with its young, and Lilith to run into the desert. This has been interpreted as chopping down the Sumerians' 'world' tree, which at the time was the centre of the ancient Near East.

The 13th-century Cabbala text, the *Book of Zohar* (The Book of Radiance – a commentary on the Jewish holy books) describes Lilith with the body of a beautiful woman, while below the navel she was a flaming

Detail from Dante Gabriel Rossetti's watercolour painting of Lileth. The accompanying epigraph of 1881 refers to 'The witch he loved before the gift of Eve.'

fire. As Adam's cast-off bride, she was relegated to the wilderness and credited with demonic sexuality. To many people today, her story is symbolic of the repression of the feminine and of the link between Satan and the flesh of women. Lilith was sometimes depicted as a snake with a woman's head, sometimes offering the apple to Adam or Eve. Described as a succubus who came to solo sleepers in erotic form, she attracted the old epithets (namely, harlot) for powerful sexual goddesses who came to be demonized in the new social structures of the day, with her sexuality damned rather than divinized.

Cabbala and the sacred body

The hidden oral Jewish tradition known as Cabbala, which became more prominent in the Middle Ages following the dissemination of the *Book of Zohar* in the 14th and 15th centuries, took on a strongly erotic element, considering sexuality the key to unlocking the secrets of the Divine. According to scholar Andrew Harvey, this mystical path to God was described as the 'jewels of the Heavenly Bride'.

The Zohar describes Divine Spirit as the light at the centre of creation, which radiates through successive spheres and is imagined as a Tree of Life. Nature is described as the garment of God. God is represented by a system of ten spheres (sephirot), which symbolize different aspects of God. The Shekhina was identified with the Malchut sphere, which is female in essence and symbolizes the female sexual organs and the beloved celebrated in the Song of Songs. Her lover was identified with God's foundation – also the phallus or male essence. The Song of Songs thus became a description of divine eroticism.

Some Cabbalists, in common with Tantric Buddhists and Hindus, regard the entire world as an expression of divine love-making. Therefore divinity and the world are mutually interdependent. This is to say that the Infinite comes to know itself through sexual union. It also implies that the sexual comes to know itself through union with consciousness – an esoteric purpose of sacred sex.

Jewish mystics, or Cabbalists, described the innermost essence of God as endless (En Sof) and described ten progressive emanations, or sephirots, such as compassion, grace and judgement.

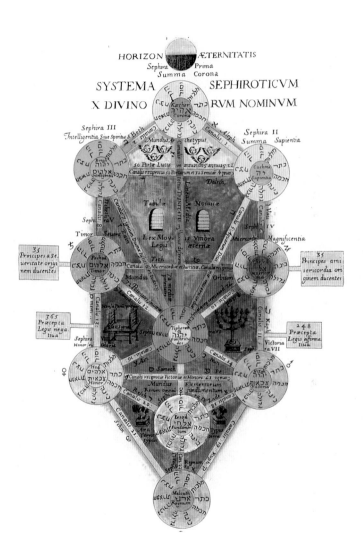

The Song of Songs

This biblical text is a supremely erotic exploration of divine union:

I am the rose of Sharon, and the lily of the valleys.
As the lily among thorns, so is my love among the daughters.
As the apple tree among the trees of the wood, so is my beloved
among the sons. I sat down under his shadow with great delight,
and his fruit was sweet to my taste.
He brought me to the banqueting house, and his banner
over me was love.
Stay me with flagons, comfort me with apples: for I am sick of love.
His left hand is under my head, and his right hand
doth embrace me.
I charge you, O ye daughters of Jerusalem, by the roes,
and by the hinds
of the field, that ye stir not up, nor awake my love, till he please.
The voice of my beloved! Behold, he cometh leaping upon the
mountains, skipping upon the hills.
My beloved is like a roe or a young hart: behold, he standeth
behind our wall, he looketh forth at the windows, showing
himself through the lattice.
My beloved spake, and said unto me, Rise up, my love,
my fair one, and come away. For, lo, the winter is past,
the rain is over and gone; the flowers appear on the earth;
the time of the singing of birds is come, and the voice
of the turtle is heard in our land;

The fig tree putteth forth her green figs, and the vines
with the tender grape give a good smell.
Arise, my love, my fair one, and come away.
O my dove, that art in the clefts of the rock, in the secret places
of the stairs, let me see thy countenance, let me hear thy voice;
for sweet is thy voice, and thy countenance is comely.
Take us the foxes, the little foxes, that spoil the vines:
for our vines have tender grapes.
My beloved is mine, and I am his: he feedeth among the lilies.
Until the day break, and the shadows flee away, turn,
my beloved, and be thou like a roe or a young hart
upon the mountains of Bether.

Song of Solomon, Chapter 2, King James Version

The world tree

The motif of the tree has a long history – from the shamanic cultures of the northern steppes, to the native americans. A potent symbol for connecting earth and heaven, the world tree has strong roots reaching down to the depths of the earth while the branches reach up to the heavens and embrace the sky, forming a bridge to the world above. This tree is a potent symbol of the fruitful relationship between heaven and earth, serpent and bull, goddess and consort. Trees found in the ancient Near East such as figs, palm, cypress, olive and apple trees, were planted in sanctuaries. In the tradition of the garden of Eden, the tree of life and knowledge symbolically offered both immortality and enlightenment. In early mythologies, trees were equated with the life force. Their seasonal cycle of flowering, leafing, fruiting and seeming decay during the winter months, followed by renewal and apparent rebirth each spring, provided a metaphor for the seasons of human life. Its regenerative power thus enables the soul to be reborn and return to the land of the living once more.

Many cultures still believe in a life after death, or an other world populated by spirits and disembodied souls. The tree can be seen as the threshold to the spirit realm, and in some regions it was customary to plant a tree directly on a person's grave, to incorporate the soul of the deceased. Tending the tree keeps the spirit sustained, wherever it is.

Stone lattice work at a 16th century mosque in Ahmehdabad, India, shows a sinuous tree entwining a statuesque palm, rather like a caduceus.

Serpent power

The serpent was a symbol of divine wisdom in ancient times. One of the defining motifs of the Christian tradition of the fall from paradise is Eve's temptation by the snake offering a bite from the tree of knowledge. Snakes have long been associated with trance states and seen as messengers from another world, and the serpent has also been seen as a form of the great goddess, ever-dying and being renewed, just as the serpent sloughs off its old skin and emerges renewed. The ancient Egyptian goddess Renenutet, depicted as a woman with the head of a cobra, was associated with gaining a 'true name' at the moment of birth – a power name that represented the essential nature of that human.

States of trance

Snakes were also symbols of prophetic power, since they were associated with the hissing sound emitted at the Delphic Oracle (see page 58) and several of the sibyls of the ancient world. The sound of a snake hissing was a definite sign of possession by a deity – or of entering a trance state in which one could inhabit the world of the deity and gather precious knowledge of this world.

Scholar Peter Kingsley describes a trance state as a state that could be called a dream, but isn't an ordinary dream. This quality of awakened awareness is key to spiritual traditions throughout the world, where the mind is turned within.

In ancient Greek practices, trance was used by initiates to enter a state of receptivity to the knowledge drawn from the realm of the gods –

Ancient Greek accounts of incubation mention the sound of snakes –
the sign of impending trance. This mosaic shows a spiral and snake.

Eve and the snake depicted in Aksum's old St Mary of Zion church, Ethiopia; below: the ourobouros.

or more usually goddesses. This was the process of mystery, in which sacred knowledge was accessed during trance. Incubation (sleeping in a sacred area to invite a dream or revelation) was an established mystery technique, through which the initiate could gain direct experience of the deeper knowledge of reality.

These ritual trips to the underworld parallel Indian yogic traditions. In India, the awakened reality called Samadhi is also known as bliss, and

considered the goal of personal transformation on the spiritual path. Meditation and yoga are waking techniques in which revelation is invited, or consciousness is prepared to receive revelation.

Other cultures looked to the shaman, as representative of the transpersonal world that underpins our daily reality, to shape shift in order to travel this alternative reality, psychically process knowledge and bring back messages from their travels.

17th-century miniature shows an ascetic yogi with snakes – symbolic of the serpent energy he has awakened through yoga practise.

Kundalini

Kundalini comes from the Sanskrit word for 'coiled', and is seen as a goddess energy in everyone, which needs to be awakened and developed in order to realize spiritual potential. Yogis describe a subtle anatomy through which energy moves when awakened by yogic and ritual practices, to revitalize the body with spiritual energy and bring about the spiritual realization that the world is pure energy, and that each individual is at one with this energy.

Kundalini is described as coiled up at the base of the spine within the energy centre (the chakra at the base of the spine).

Through meditation and other ritual practices the serpent energy can be stimulated to climb through the several energy centres, leading to different levels of awakening and mystical experience. The goal is for this energy to reach the energy centre at the top of the head, which opens the human consciousness to the transcendental realms of bliss (see page 176).

Western Thinking

Sin, Sex and Freud

The rules of sex

The huge social control of Christianity paralyzed certain areas of inquiry in Western thought – from 400 until at least 1000 CE – and attitudes to women and sexuality have only relaxed relatively recently. According to Reay Tannahill's book *Sex in History*, many Christian rules regarding sex originated in the punitive Hebrew laws dating from the time of the Old Testament and these have been applied to the control of sexuality and women in particular for over 1,500 years. The model of hellfire and damnation favoured by the Catholic Church, together with a terrifying apparatus of control, meant that most of the population dared not step out of line. Men and women were certainly afraid of sin, and some sexual transgressions such as sodomy were punishable by death – which in the Middle Ages was always by sadistic methods. Vestiges of older matriarchal cultures, where wise women, healers and midwives were respected members of the community, were particularly attacked.

Regulating coitus

Around the 8th century the Church developed the enormously strict system for regulating sexual behaviour that blighted the Middle Ages. A series of penitential books detailed unacceptable behaviours, such as fornication, sodomy and even masturbation, as well as the penances due for infringement. The Church went on to reduce the number of days on which married couples could legitimately have sex to just a few months of the year, making it clear that its control entered even into private bedrooms.

Eve, the Serpent and Death by Renaissance artist Hans Baldung Grien (c. 1510). The serpent is sometimes depicted as a woman, Eve is ensnared, while here Adam represents death.

The Catholic attitude to female sexuality became mixed up with the idea of witchcraft, with women seen as temptresses. Lust and sex had long been associated with the original sin of Adam and Eve or were regarded as the mark of the devil; after the time of St Augustine (see page 51) this view was part of mainstream Christian theology.

Towards the end of the Middle Ages, Pope Innocent VIII issued a papal Bull against witchcraft which Gordon Rattray Taylor summarized as 'far more preoccupied with impotence cases, fertility troubles and crop failures than with pagan worship or magical acts.' The famous witch hunter's handbook, the *Malleus Maleficarum*, written in 1486, claimed, 'All witchcraft

119

This engraving from the Compendium Malleficarum, *1626, illustrates sorcerers and witches who were supposed to ritually kiss the backside of Satan, every sabbath. 'Arse-kissing' was the foul act of a follower of Satan and, as such, was an abhorrence.*

comes from carnal lust,' which in women is 'insatiable'. It was a basic assumption that any witch had had intercourse with Satan, and in the popular imagination such women were nightly cavorting with incubi.

While the vast bulk of witchcraft accusations were fabrications, a small group of pagans may have continued a secret worship of the Horned One, sometimes known as Cernunnos, and occasionally depicted as a horned serpent. With a pedigree stretching back to ancient times, these rites may have been ecstatic in character and, like certain other pagan religions such as the ecstatic cult of the wine-god Dionysus, may have culminated in the hieros gamos of ritual union.

The horned god, Cernunnos, with sacred animals, found on a 1st-century BCE silver cauldron in Denmark.

Courtly love and the Cathars

In France in medieval times, a tradition of courtly love sprang up that has influenced our modern notion of romantic love to this day. Each troubadour extolled the virtues of his muse, a woman he wooed without expectation of starting a relationship; what was important was the idealization and longing. The rules governing 'courtly love' were collected into a *Treatise of Love* c. 1186, compiled by the Persian philosopher and mystic Ibn Sina (Avicenna).

The relationship between higher-status women and their suitors was rarely consummated, but produced a flowering of notions of honour, chivalry and etiquette, and reinspired a chaste notion of love. Courtly love, during its early centuries, was suited to the courtly class. But for the bourgeois of the Reformation, it was too demanding: eventually it metamorphosed into the model of courting followed by a romantic marriage that we recognize today.

The very same area that gave birth to courtly love (Provence and the Languedoc in the south of France) produced a religious movement known as Catharism.

A student declares his love to a noble lady, miniature from Le Chansonnier de Paris *(song book), c. 1280–1315*

Cathars were expelled from the city of Carcasonne in Southern France in 1209, by the army of Simon de Montfort. Thousands of Cathars were massacred as heretics in the 13th centuries.

Both movements emphasized the feminine and radically elevated the spiritual value of women, producing both secular and spiritual alternatives to the orthodoxy of the day.

The Cathars followed a Gnostic vision of the creation, where the world was imperfect and could be redeemed by the spiritual seeker living a life of purity. Devoted to spiritual enlightenment, they rejected the trappings of the corrupt Catholic Church, and also marriage. Men and women both conducted services in peasant areas. Calling themselves the 'good people', they followed a simple life of vegetarianism, prayer and non-violence. The Church founded the Inquisition partially to stamp out the 'heresy' and proceeded to systematically wipe out the Cathars, which they did by 1244.

The Middle Ages and magical thinking

In the Middle Ages, the soul was not just an insubstantial spiritual entity associated with the individual; the earth, too, was considered to have a soul, as well as the planets. Soul imbued the universe and everything in it, so that the smallest part of the universe, the microcosm, was considered to be subject to the same principles as the whole, the macrocosm. Everything in the macrocosm was connected with everything else, so that soul was both inside a thing or a person and outside it, part of the cosmos.

These days, we commonly distinguish between classes of substance (man and planet are different types of object) and between man and matter, psyche and substance, but medieval man had a very different world view. The soul was an integrated unity of spirit, psyche and matter; thus rituals could be applied to one part in order to affect the whole. We now term this kind of thinking, in which coincidental relationships between things are part of explanatory systems, 'magical'.

Magical thinking is key to understanding rituals such as the hieros gamos (sacred marriage), in which a mortal stood in for a divine figure, and in so doing, she became divine. Everything she did impacted on the realm of the divine, as well as on the world of man.

Understanding that style of thinking is also important for comprehending the quest of the alchemists – to investigate and reveal the divine realm through chemically transforming material substances. At the same time they aimed to transform consciousness through transforming matter.

Woodcut from the alchemical treatise Rosarium Philosophorum
depicting Holy Wisdom being crowned by God and the Pope.

The divorce of body and soul

Social historian Roy Porter's book *Flesh in the Age of Reason* tells how individual consciousness and the awareness of that consciousness, was refined over centuries from its roots in the command at Dephi to 'know thyself', through the Christian idea of a unique, eternal soul inextricably bound up in the body, into the Renaissance, with an increasingly materialistic perspective. After the Reformation, which established Protestantism in northern Europe in the early 16th century, the West began to struggle more violently to loosen the grip of the Catholic Church and became attracted to the light of reason.

Cartesian duality

From the time of Descartes (1596–1650), matter was defined as either inanimate or as imbued with spirit (or spirit-psyche). Descartes split the previously unified world soul into the inanimate and that which animated it, firmly separating inner from outer, and soul from matter. This is what we call a dualistic world view. Since then, the principle of Eros and its association with divine wisdom has largely disappeared from descriptions of the natural world. Descartes came to the conclusion that only man could know himself. This was the start of our contemporary elevation of the mind and consciousness, replacing the archaic idea of soul.

An increasingly secular style of reason underpins our contemporary ideal of the individual as rational and self-determining. The notion of an individual 'self' now preoccupies Western philosophy. Once the relationship between mind and soul was uncoupled, that between mind

In this 1826 frontispeice to the Works of Aristotle *Wisdom, in the form of the goddess Sophia, appears before the philosopher couped up in his study, her nakedness symbolizing truth and beauty.*

and body became the new arena for investigation. The fledgling discipline of anatomy, which emerged from Padua (Italy) in the 15th century, could only emerge once the body was shorn of its sacred soul, and meant that physicians could legitimately cut open a body, leading to the death of old humoral ideas about how the body worked. Science has since arisen in opposition to religious ideologies – in no small part due to the persecution of leading scientists such as Galileo; our bodies are now no longer inseparable from the macrocosm, and our sexuality has been released from the claims of the soul. Materialist attitudes have further alienated us from the field that also once gave erotic experience a holistic meaning.

Sex in the Victorian Era

Some social historians comment that from the Dark Ages up to the development of modern medicine, and in particular with the discovery of effective means of treating sexually transmitted diseases, sexual pleasure was blighted by 1000 years of poverty. But poverty, along with the repression of sex in the Victorian era, led to widespread prostitution. There were street-walkers (both amateur and professional), courtesans and kept women. Marriage was about creating strategic alliances, acquiring property and raising children to continue the family name, while mistresses were for sexual adventure for those who could afford it. Many such women felt they were better off financially than if they were wives or servants, and attitudes in the Georgian era were more liberal as regards women's sexual status than they were by the late Victorian era, with the rise in a model of affectionate, companionable marriage.

In 1839, in London, a city of two million inhabitants, there were estimated to be up to 80,000 prostitutes. These figures may have been grossly over-estimated, yet in the post-industrial world, prostitution appears largely connected with the needs of the urban poor to access quick money; in the Victorian era, which was a time of rapid and widespread industrialization, there were often few resources available to poor women in times of financial hardship to keep them from the dreaded debtors' prison or the workhouse.

Orientalist Lord Leighton's 1862 painting of a chambermaid, Odalisque. He was part of a group of Victorian artists who romanticized the lives of servants and entertainers, as middle-class mores restricted their own.

Encounters with the East:
The 'Hindoo' Erotic

Richard Burton (1821–90) was a maverick explorer who turned his attention to the sex life of 'the Hindoos' in the British Raj where, by virtue of his command of the language and customs of the people, he was tasked with reporting whether British officers were frequenting male brothels.

Richard Burton was a colourful example of Victorians who 'went native', throwing themselves into an exploration of exotic cultures in a style that inspired the emerging discipline of social anthropology. While employed by the colonial bureaucracy, his reputation was tarnished amongst his peers by the uninhibited presentation and discussion of his findings.

Shortly after arriving in India at the age of 21, he took up with a Nautch dancer, and discovered a very different attitude toward sexuality, which suited him. The temple carvings at Elephantine Island, where he saw detailed depictions of sexual acts that seemed to evidence a celebratory attitude to Eros, were in stark contrast to the repressed and distinctly unerotic attitudes and behaviour of his fellow colonialists, who were renowned amongst the Indian women as lousy lovers.

While many British officers frequented the prostitutes or took local mistresses and consigned the offspring of such unions to orphanages, Burton got more involved in the language and culture of India. Not only did he translate the *Kama Sutra*, to ambivalent acclaim back in England, but he also added a commentary. He wrote that most men appeared to

The explicit content of this 19th century Indian miniature is at odds with much contemporary Victorian art of the West.

ignore the feelings of women, and failed to prepare them for sexual intercourse. Apparently, British men were renowned for their lack of sensuality. Burton discovered that India had a rich and sensual tradition of the erotic that he determined to explore.

Soul mates

From the late 17th century, there was an outpouring of publications
about sex, some of which remained in print for centuries. *Aristotle's
Masterpiece*, published in 1684 (and not, of course, written by the
ancient Greek philosopher), a compendium of assorted facts and hearsay
but broadly about reproduction, was enormously popular. *Conjugal Love*
(1686), penned in French by Nicolas Venette, explored sexual physiology
and tried to incorporate emerging
notions of more companionate
marriage, arguing that sex was
preferable in a conjugal
relationship.

From around 1750, with the
influence of Enlightenment ideas
that described human nature as a
state of innocence, formed by life
experiences, erotic desire began
to be seen as natural and good –
while the ascetic life and the
scourging of the flesh among
fervent Catholic sects seemed
distorted. The idea of original sin
and the associated shame and guilt
around sexuality began to lift. The
Romantic movement dismissed the

earlier liberal sexual practices, with the unashamedly public proliferation of pornography and prostitution, as gross, and was responsible for a trend in romanticizing women and love, as well as sexual love. Around the 1890s there were debates about a more elevated 'psychic' kind of love than that offered by the conjugal relationship – what we would recognize as 'soul mates'. A few philosophically inclined salons explored the ecstatic language of sexuality. Catholic Charles Kingsley (1819–75) wrote about sex as a God-given pleasure within the marriage bed, while poet Coventry Patmore (1823–96) described sex as metaphor for religious experience;

Patmore appears to have practised retention of ejaculation and regarded abstinence as essential to a good sex life.

According to Lesley Hall, researcher at the Wellcome Library, the emphasis on abstinence within an ideal of temperate indulgence is note-worthy during this period, and not gratifying desire was advocated to develop a more refined sexuality.

Armida is a Saracen sorceress, sent to bewitch a Christian soldier, Rinaldo, in this 1812 painting by Francesco Hayez. Temptation is seen as being put in the way of this god-fearing Christian by a wicked non-believer.

The Wandering Womb

Hysteria was a common complaint diagnosed in women for hundreds of years in Western Europe, peaking in the Victorian era. Described as being due to a 'wandering womb', from the time of Hippocrates on, hysteria was blamed for a host of 'nervous' symptoms.

The Greek physician Galen had described hysteria in the 2nd century CE as a disease of the womb caused by sexual deprivation in passionate women: it was often diagnosed in virgins, nuns, widows and, occasionally, married women. Appropriately, a favoured Victorian remedy recommended for these ardent women was sex – but if the woman was unmarried, genital or pelvic massage might be recommended as a therapeutic technique. From around the 1500s, doctors might be called on to produce an orgasm manually – although, given the unconducive setting, it could take hours to achieve the 'hysterical paroxysm' needed to decongest the womb. In an anti-masturbation era, the solution was to invent massage devices designed to shorten treatment time to minutes.

Although hysteria is no longer considered a disease, the word has passed into common parlance to describe a reactive and labile over-emotionality. Many cases that would once have been labelled hysteria were reclassified by Sigmund Freud (see page 142) as anxiety neuroses. The term 'neurosis' was adopted by the emerging pseudo-science of psychoanalysis, which has taken hold of the popular imagination in a big way. It is now used to refer to mild but pervasive anxiety and self-absorbed analytical thinking – but still applied to women much more frequently than to men.

Among the Victorians madness in women was thought to be inextricably linked with sexuality. This woman experiences hysteria (from the Greek for womb).

The birth of sexology

The scientific study of sexual behaviour began in the 19th century with researchers such as Havelock Ellis (1859–1939), who was the first to investigate sexual behaviour and attitudes in a non-judgemental way, discussing desires and diverse experiences as on a natural continuum of behaviour. In Ellis's vision of the ideal sexual life, periodical abstinence was essential, preventing pleasure from ever becoming stale or a banal routine. He also did not believe that desire had to be satisfied immediately it arose. Ellis himself remained celibate. Researchers such as Ellis challenged prejudices about homosexuality, which was classed as an inversion of normal heterosexual desire. Extensive prohibitions about 'self-abuse' only changed very slowly, in the 20th century, as masturbation finally came onto the sex-education agenda.

It was Marie Stopes (1880–1958) who finally replaced the notion of women as having as lusty a sexuality as men with the need for 'mutual adjustment', skill, tenderness, tact and patience. The first in a tradition that has spawned many of today's 'agony aunts', Stopes received many letters from 1918 onwards expressing a deep idealism about the potential of the physical relationship within marriage, as well as a profound disappointment with the reality of their sex lives. Stopes' books, including *Enduring Passion* (1928), were the first to advocate 'good sex', and promote an awareness of women's need for sexual stimulation and the importance of a sensitive and accomplished lover.

Through the growth of marital manuals by birth control reformers such as Stopes (who worked tirelessly to improve sexual knowledge for

Marie Stopes (1880–1958), a fervent campaigner for birth control, and later a tireless sex educator.

married couples), sexologist Kinsey (whose research method involved comprehensive questionnaires of large numbers of men and women), and then Masters and Johnson (who studied sexual arousal and response cycles in a 'laboratory setting' using male and female prostitutes), the stage was set for the work of the founders of modern sex therapy.

Based on personal reports, interviews and observations, this new sexology was regarded as deeply radical at the time. However, the legacy of all this sex-survey research has been to establish norms about sex that are almost exclusively performance-oriented – with intercourse and orgasm heading the list. While these norms are suitable for measuring physiological behaviour and response, none of them takes into account the subjective issues that are so vital to sexual pleasure and wellbeing: trust, communication, empathy, intimacy and the spiritual connections inherent in sexual desire and satisfaction. Sex therapy can still be limited by an overly mechanistic and medical approach.

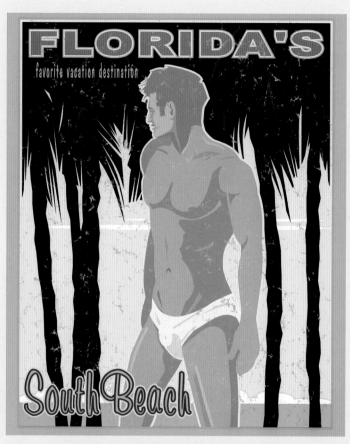

Male sexuality became an acceptable means of advertising the charms of 20th century holiday resorts as in this 1950s poster.

Homosexuality and 1950s Research

Some time in the 1950s the distinction between 'sex' and 'gender' became significant in society; and the notion of gender contributed to the emergence of a more sophisticated discussion of the differences between men and women.

Researchers realized that homosexuality was neither a perversion of normal desire, as earlier sex researchers had asserted, nor a definite biological or psychological condition. Homosexuality referred to an identity attached to the individual by others or by themselves. In contemporary society, the prevalence of identity politics means many people choose to define their identity in relation to the object of their sexual desire.

Just as masculinity and femininity are socially constructed roles that men and women use to define themselves – or not – so homosexuality is a social role. You can choose to describe yourself as homosexual, making your sexual behaviour into an identity – or others may do so without your consent.

This is an important distinction, because the actual sexual behaviours of people who define themselves as heterosexual or homosexual might not be much different – but the way these individuals present themselves in society may be. The choices individuals have made about this have varied throughout history, depending on the possible consequences of those choices.

Rise of the medical paradigm

Anyone who grows up in a contemporary Western culture is conditioned to think of sex as intercourse – the words are often used synonymously. Current research shows intercourse may be brilliantly designed to cater to male genital pleasure, but many women feel dissatisfied by sex with such low expectations. The trend in lay and medical circles is to regard sexual dissatisfaction as a disease. Any kind of sex in which either party doesn't function according to a pretty limited template of foreplay, intercourse, orgasm is now treated as a dysfunction. The fact that women are not particularly excited about this format is treated as evidence of another huge category of dysfunction – female desire disorders.

Since the 1960s we have taken it for granted that our attitudes to sex are more liberal – but while it's certainly much more acceptable to grab sex with whoever and whenever you can, the ways we talk and think about sex tend to be limited. Contemporary manuals on sex are obsessed with positions, birth control, prevention of sexually transmitted disease and where to go for help with sexual dysfunctions, but there is insufficient debate about what sex means to us and the ways we could change its function within a relationship.

Sigmund Freud, originally a neurologist, can be credited with creating an intellectual climate in which understanding the role of our sexual drives and their relationship to our bodies and minds was key. By World War II, the impact of Freudian ideas in psychiatry and psychology was widely accepted; they have since permeated sociology, anthropology, history and literary criticism – and, of course, popular culture.

In Western culture the physical act of intercourse tends to be seen as the ultimate goal in a relationship rather than a means to emotionally connect with your partner.

Freud's theory of sexuality

Freud famously did not know what women wanted, and also regarded many neurotic (women) patients as incurable. Psychoanalysis has its roots in the Victorian understanding of women's sexuality as fundamentally hysterical.

Freud developed his theory of sexuality at the end of the 19th century, based on current thinking in neurology that suggested psychosomatic symptoms were based on blocked or frustrated sexual drives, giving rise to all sorts of neurotic problems. He generalized theories derived from his work with hysterics to argue that the sex principle was universal, and furthermore, that it underlay and motivated all human drives and internal psychic conflicts.

Unconscious drives

Sigmund Freud believed that people are driven by two conflicting central desires – the life drive (libido or Eros) and the death drive. Freud described the aim of Eros as 'to establish [psychological] unity' within the unconscious. By locating such drives in the unconscious, where they were out of conscious control (unless an analyst helped to excavate them), Freud established a whole new way of thinking that underpins modern thinking about sex and the self. First, he restated the idea that sexuality is a defining feature of human consciousness. In assigning some of our behaviour to drives outside our control, we cannot always be held responsible for our actions. Sex was not necessarily about awareness, but could be powered by an instinctual drive. The libido was seen as a primal

Freud's study – birthplace of free association – saying whatever comes into your mind while 'on the couch'. This technique revealed surprising links to unconscious drives – often sexual.

force motivating much of our conscious and unconscious behaviour, and one whose repression is fraught with perils, even as control of our sexual impulses is deemed crucial to the process of 'civilization'.

Freud argued that humans are born 'polymorphously perverse' meaning any number of objects could be a source of pleasure initially. His observations that amorphous sexual experiences were progressively channelled into an acceptable (hetero) sexual identity at critical developmental periods, starting from infancy, were hugely radical.

His concept of sexuality was of something much more plastic: like the rest of our brain function, it could be modelled and remodelled over time, depending on what influences someone was exposed to and how they responded. Such ideas suggest that our sexuality is nowhere near as fixed as we imagine – and there is actually the potential to change the object of our desire, the form our desire takes and just about everything about the way we experience it. Freud believed that everyone is fundamentally bisexual and becomes socialized into a sexual role – a completely radical perspective.

Breakdown or breakthrough

In 1888 Freud had proposed that neurons that 'fire together wire together', implying you can strenghten the connections between love and sex – although this statement properly belongs to modern neuroscience. His technique of free association – where his client would say whatever came into his or her mind without inhibition – meant that the traumatic memories that produced neurotic symptoms could be recovered and released as they came into consciousness.

'Transpersonal' is the term used by psychoanalysts for the mystical drive towards expanded consciousness (beyond the usual boundaries of ego, and time and space). Freud saw attempts to channel sexual energy into a transpersonal union as neurotic and immature, thus casting the mystical search for the transpersonal as regressive. In his book *On Hysteria*, psychoanalyst Christopher Bollas described the conversion of sexual desire into a desire for spiritual union or communion as a de-sexualization of desire, which harks back to the need of the hysteric to pour out romantic aspirations into idealized fantasies.

Freud's theories pathologized female sexuality and saw women as deeply envious of the phallus.

French neurologist Jean-Martin Charcot (1825–93) proposed ideas that suggested hysteria had a psychological causation that included trauma. He suggested hypnotism as a suitable treatment.

Jung and gender theory

Carl Jung (1876–1961) disagreed with Freud's exclusive emphasis on sexuality, and his quite different theories – some of which embraced eastern philosophy – have had a lasting influence on thinking about both psychology and psycho-spirituality. As many sacred sex practitioners use Jung's concepts to describe the sacred marriage, I will touch on the way he has shaped a gendered understanding of personality. Jung developed a concept of complementary-gendered attributes in each individual, that needed to be integrated in order to develop a more complete personality. Jung associated women's psychology with the principle of Eros (love) as psychic relatedness, while men are associated with Logos (the word), as reason. Harking back to the ancient Greeks, Logos was conceived of as the world order, and referred to the light and reason observable within chaos. From the time of the neo-Platonist Philo on, Logos was given more respect than the feminine quality of Wisdom (Sophia), and became associated with Christianity and monotheism. Like the Gnostics and other mystics, Jung agreed that the feminine aspect of love and wisdom needed to be reintegrated with the masculine attributes of reason.

Soul healing

While the ancients had long talked about the animus or soul, Jung assigned different-gendered aspects of the soul to men and women. He described the anima as the repressed feminine side of a man, and the animus as the unconscious male principle in a woman. According to Jung, both aspects were crucial to self development – and fundamental to a

Jung's theory says every individual has masculine and feminine attributes. The two must be integrated for that individual to develop a well-rounded personality

truly integrated self. Jungian analysts have described the way individuals and couples explore these aspects through relationships with the opposite sex. The idea of 'projection' describes the ways in which we identify our own styles of behaving in our partners, rather than acknowledging those same qualities as aspects of our own character. Part of the challenge in a relationship is to take back these projections, and work on integrating ourselves, rather than on trying to change our partner. Allowing a man to

This statue by Canova depicts Eros awakening the lifeless Psyche (who stands for the human soul) with a kiss. Romantic love begins with idealized passion.

Woman are traditionally associated with Eros and intimacy.

express his feminine side and a woman to express her masculine side allows for greater personal growth and understanding and for a relationship to grow into a complementary union.

Eros is the 'desire for wholeness', which is necessary for us to know ourselves. By understanding 'passionate love' and the 'desire for wholeness' as 'psychic relatedness', Jung also characterized the desire for love as a desire for interconnection.

According to the popularized application of Jung's theory, a negative animus (masculine principle) could lead to a domineering, opinionated, egotistical and controlling slant to one's personality. A negative anima (feminine principle) is denigrated as making women moody, bitchy, controlling, needy and demanding. For men, wishing to integrate their feminine side means reclaiming emotions, instinctual responses and intuitive connection with others – the quality of empathy. For women, integrating the masculine side means reclaiming their independence, focused direction and sense of personal power.

Calling up material from your unconscious mind can enable you to integrate the masculine and feminine sides of your personality.

Exploring your animus

The feminine is often considered to represent intense emotionalism, dynamic energy and magnetic attraction. In esoteric traditions the masculine principle often represents incisive awareness and reason.

Exploring the negative sides of our personality is considered an essential part of self-development. Jung suggests we integrate light and dark aspects and that it may be necessary to claim the positive aspects of your own gender before working with its opposite – especially if you experience a sense of shame or inadequacy for any reason.

Receiving the vision

One way of exploring these archetypes is to evoke them with a visualization. You may have completely different associations to those mentioned above, and a guided visualization may help you to discover your own associations. Active imagination has long been used to invoke the Self, and to call up material from your unconscious mind. Reflecting on aspects of your Self can help you to integrate them. Active imagination is an important technique used by Jungians to access the contents of the unconscious mind, revealed through dreams and images that arise when you are in a receptive state. The key is to exert as little influence as possible on these mental images as they unfold. You need to observe things in your mind's eye, rather than consciously fill the scene with what you want to happen. You can then respond genuinely to these changes. Spend time conjuring up associations to the idea of your inner masculine – or feminine. Change the gender of the psychic component as needed.

Integrate your inner male and female

Get to know your wise side

Use this meditation as a starting point to explore your unconscious – and what your own inner animus might be like.

1 Sit comfortably with eyes closed and allow your breath to deepen and slow down. Imagine you are sitting in your favourite place – it could be your garden, a forest or a beach.

2 Allow the light, warmth and tranquillity to permeate your being for a few minutes. Feel your senses engage in the natural world.

3 Invite Sophia – the wise aspect of yourself that guides you and keeps you safe – to join you. Be aware that this could be in the form of awareness, an insight, a sensation or a vision.

4 Once manifest, ask Sophia to show you her male aspect – your inner male.

5 As he appears, notice what he looks like and anything else about him. Notice what qualities he embodies. Is there something he wants to communicate to you? Imaginatively open yourself to receiving any message.

6 Ask him about the function of your inner male and its purpose in your life.

7 If he wishes to offer you an object, accept it graciously. This could be a symbol, or a quality, that you take into yourself like a seed. Find a creative way to incorporate this masculine principle inside yourself.

8 Slowly come back to normal consciousness and spend a few moments reflecting on the message – if there was one.

Encounter with the transpersonal

Jungian perspectives have permeated psychology and firmly encourage individuals to identify with inner rather than outer goals, which can be seen as something of a return to the Delphic dictum to know oneself – albeit wrapped up in a distinctly individualistic ideology. Jung expanded

the study of the unconscious into a wide model that encompassed a spiritual perspective, while still remaining acceptable to the contemporary world of the individualistic, self-determining individual.

The willingness to let go of specific goals and allow ourselves to surrender to impersonal forces requires a big shift in attitude. For Jung, this is part of the encounter of the individual with the transpersonal realm – the term psychoanalysts use when referring to the spiritual.

Magical thinking

The natural world makes no distinction about whether our lives are worthwhile, or whether we deserve misfortune, disease or suffering. Such things are arbitrary, often happening for no discernible reason. Rather than resenting any perceived injustice in what has happened, it may be more appropriate to accept that some forces lie outside our personal control. A spiritual perspective might help you access wisdom and get your life force moving again in the wake of a set back.

Anthropological studies talk about pre-scientific ways of understanding life as magical – relating the things that happen in life to the movement of transpersonal energies through myriad interconnections. Reconnecting with more instinctual levels of wisdom often brings a sense of being interconnected with other human beings – our essential similarity – and with all life forms. This helps us to place the personal challenges that we all face on our individual journey through life in a broader context.

The shri yantra mandala, in which the upward-pointing triangles of the feminine receive the downward-pointing triangles of the masculine can be used in meditation to balance the masculine and feminine and clear negative energies.

Relationship as a crucible

In modern psychological terms, the sacred wedding can be seen as a crucible in which two individuals in an intimate relationship bring together both the issues that they are aware of and those that lurk in the dark. Jung called these aspects the shadow. These unpleasant, argumentative and self-righteous sides of ourselves usually surface in a relationship of any depth.

The crucible of relationship is one in which intense feelings and passions – no matter how wrong-headed – are ground down and undergo transformation in order to emerge reconstituted. The transformation of these primal energies creates something new – something based on an understanding of each other, in which communication is not always considerate or self-sacrificing, but can be passionate in fighting for the right to remain different to each other. Two figures emerge more differentiated, and therefore with more respect for one another.

Accept the shadow side

The hieros gamos (sacred marriage) is not just about marrying heart and mind, but also about marrying the light and shadow. A modern sacred wedding is about awareness, empathy, joy and bliss. In order to reach the level of the sacred marriage, however, most couples know they have to pass through periods of intense or petty warfare, in which resentment or meanness prevent them from simply going with the flow. These emotions are just energy – and there is usually a great deal in any close relationship, although often it is locked up in efforts to prevent the free

The crucible of a relationship allows couples to acknowledge character traits they may prefer to ignore, and to emerge stronger, and with more respect for one another.

flow of energies between partners. What lies in the shadow is often the parts of ourselves that we don't like; however, wholeness implies acknowledging those undervalued parts of ourselves. While we may judge ourselves as chaotic, demanding, selfish, unpleasant or ugly, all these uncomfortable aspects still need some space in our lives. If we try to cut them off we risk losing power and passion, a source of creative expression and unbridled energy. Feeling emotionally cold or indifferent is often a

sign that we are cut off from the source of our vitality – often because such emotions are deemed unacceptable. Becoming aggressive and attacking is another response to unacknowledged emotion. These inarticulated emotions may come up as we struggle to reclaim a sense of identity; a sense of who we are and what we want. The archetypal language of the sacred wedding repeatedly emphasizes the union of the split aspects of masculinity and femininity. One of the challenges of the

sacred context of this wedding is for men to step into their innate divinity and embody the divine masculine (God), who is able to perceive and appreciate the divine feminine (Goddess) as his equal counterpart. For women struggling to find their repressed masculine side, the idea of the sacred wedding can encourage them to step into a sense of personal power through accepting their inner wisdom and the power of the divine archetype.

Jung associated women's psychology with Eros, love and relationship and men with Logos and order.

The feminine today

Contemporary Western culture lacks a strong image of the feminine in the sacred. Historically the goddess was largely supplanted by the patriarchal god of monotheistic religions such as Christianity and Judaism. This provides an unfortunate template for conflict, power struggle and subjugating others in order to impose one's own will, all contemporary social and political ills writ large across our international landscape.

Obviously, the causes of the current problems cannot be reduced to a simplistic notion of patriarchal myth, especially in view of the fact that myth and archetype are largely marginalized in modern culture. The message of the feminine archetype asks us to restore dialogue in order to heal wounded creation, acknowledge the need to internalize compassionate wisdom, and allow cycles of growth and renewal, as processes during which darkness and difficulty are reworked and transformed within the crucible of conscious awareness.

Back to nature

The consequences of a dualistic split between civilization and nature, mind and emotion, power and Eros, reason and intuition over the last few thousand years threaten to distract us from the pressing issues of our times. We need to remind ourselves that all of humanity is as interconnected as life forms are interdependent – that different viewpoints need to be heard as complementary rather than oppositional, and that nature needs to be seen as part of life rather than something to be exploited. A central issue of our times is how to rise above divisive thinking in order to work together for the common good to create a more

This 1907 painting by Gustav Klimt depicts the myth of Danaë, daughter of the King of Argos, sexually aroused by Zeus, who appears between her thighs as a golden stream.

sustainable relationship between ourselves and our resources.

While many people look to technological solutions to the many challenges that currently face us, others believe that unless the needs of planet earth are brought firmly centre stage, it may be too late for our survival as a species. These days, major shifts in social structures occur not as a result of thoughtful holistic planning, but as a by-product of a technological age spurred on by commercial endeavour and scientific enquiry.

Return of Gaia

Trying to bring us full circle, back into relationship with a natural world in which the mother goddess reigns supreme, ecologist James Lovelock coined the name of the Greek goddess Gaia to describe the scientific principle in which nature has its own self-regulating mechanisms which are essential to maintaining the best possible conditions in the atmosphere of the planet. As these mechanisms are crucial to sustaining life, Lovelock described them as nurturing. He called for a reinstatement of Gaia, arguing that without nurturing planet earth we are doomed as a species. His hypothesis was taken up in the 70s and proved useful in stimulating scientific and ecological debate, which has fed into today's concerns with the planet and sustainability. Tied up with a green ethos and the need to attend to the environmental fragility of our abused planet, the Gaia hypothesis was a wake-up call we ignore at our peril.

Namaste, an ancient Hindu salutation of welcome and honour. A modern translation is 'The spirit in me respects the spirit in you.'

Return of the feminine

The challenge that ecological awareness poses for individuals on the spiritual path is not just to awaken their own higher self but to awaken the collective consciousness of mankind, and as philosopher Ken Wilber says, to ensure that enlightened awareness is 'embraced in culture, embodied in nature, and embedded in social institutions'. Evolutionary spirituality reaffirms the Jungian belief that the principle of Eros drives the world. The principle of Eros was, and remains, a fundamentally sexual orientation towards the entire world, which emphasizes interconnection and relationship.

Goddess worship and sacred sex have moved back into the mainstream, with an explosion of sites on the Internet dedicated to sexual healing and Tantric massage. For sacred sex practitioners, Eros drives the personal path to transformation. Deeper insights and understanding gleaned from esoteric traditions both West and East make it clear that higher development entails embracing and serving the world, once you realize that the world is inseparable from one's self. The deeper realization is to go beyond the meditative state of the yogis, who have transcended mundane reality, into a bigger awareness of the fundamental interconnectedness of everything, and our current need as a culture to hold that awareness as much as possible.

In the East, disentangling the personal self from the world in order to enlighten oneself is equated with wisdom. This journey may involve descending into the realm of the goddess, or (to use more contemporary terms) the non-dual realm where material and immaterial are all one.

Discovering that all differences and reasons for separation collapse in a deeper awareness of the absolute oneness of all phenomena is necessary before returning to the world in order to help others attain the same awareness. Within the Buddhist tradition, this journey is equated with first developing love and compassion, and then integrating both qualities into a unified awareness is seen as 'the union of wisdom and compassion'.

In *Sex, Ecology, Spirituality*, philosopher Ken Wilber summarized the classic non-dual perspective in both East and West:

> *Flee the many, find the One*
> *Embrace the Many as the One*

The challenge for spiritual seekers is to gain awareness of non-duality through practices that 'open the eye of the soul', as Plato would have put it; his idea persists in the Sufi notion of 'the eye of the heart', or 'the eye of Tao' according to Taoism. The goal is to achieve an illusion-shattering wisdom that acknowledges our true transcendental nature as recognized by Hindus, Buddhists, Sufis and Christian Gnostics.

In the next chapter we shall look at the influence of Eastern traditions, and at what they have to teach us about a return to a more integrated, holistic sexuality.

Gaia theory teaches us that we are deeply interconnected – not just with other humans, but with the whole of life as an integrated and holistic system which supports, nourishes and sustains us all.

Eastern Approaches
to Sex and the Spirit

A holistic view

In the East there is an awareness of the unity and interconnectedness of all things and events as part of a cosmic whole. Whichever aspect of life you look at is considered a different manifestation of the same ultimate reality, which different traditions label according to their own system or metaphysics. According to yoga and meditative traditions, for example, the human body itself is part of a dynamic field of life and cannot be separated from it. The body is therefore fundamental to a holistic approach to self-development.

Physicist Albert Einstein (1879–1955) described a human being as:

> *'... a part of the whole that we call the universe, limited in time and space. He experiences himself, his thoughts and feelings as something separated from the rest – a kind of optical illusion of his consciousness. This illusion is a prison for us, restricting us to our personal desires and to affection for only a few people nearest us; our task must be to free ourselves from this prison by widening our circle of compassion to embrace all living beings and all of nature.'*

In Eastern philosophy, the main terms used in Hinduism and Buddhism have dynamic connotations. For instance, the word Brahman is derived from the Sanskrit root 'brh', which refers to growth. Creation is also referred to as a dance. Shiva is often depicted as a dancer. The qualities associated with cosmic energy refer to an energy that vibrates, much as contemporary physicists understand a wave form.

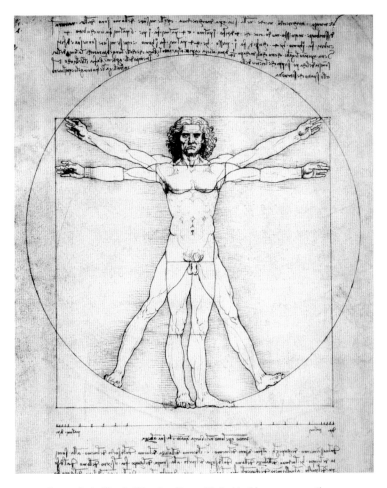

*Leonardo da Vinci's Vitruvian Man with its ideal human proportions,
projects the idea that the human body correlates to ancient geometry.*

Bronze statue of Shiva as Nataraja (lord of the dance), source of all movement within the cosmos, represented by the arch of flames.

Energy fields

Quantum physics – the world of the very small – now provides scientific explanations for the phenomena described in Eastern philosophy. The idea of waves has replaced the old model of atoms or particles. According to physicist Geoff Haselhurst, particles are not real but are formed by the overlapping of different wave forms, which gives an impression of matter. Matter can be described as the place where different wave forms meet – and this, in turn, changes the pattern of wave forms, which then ripple out to form another meeting place.

This echoes the philosophical language used by Eastern practitioners to describe our sensory perception of the world as an illusion. It is interesting that the world of physics agrees with the description offered by Hindu and Buddhist traditions of energy as the fundamental nature of the universe, in which there are only waves.

Matter as a wave

Physicist Milo Wolff's *Wave Theory of Matter* explains the way the two energy fields of individuals can interact on each other. Every time we move – and this includes the motion produced by our cognitive processes when we think – there is a change in the shapes of the waves we emit, which then flow out into the universe and cause a slight adjustment in the waves emanating from others. These effects might be minute but, as chaos theory suggests, even minimal changes can have a huge impact on the world. Our impact on other things affects the changed waves that flow back into us – so there is continual communication between all matter.

What is the spiritual path?

The esoteric traditions that we are discussing in this book favour the personal experience as a gateway to the divine. In this context, personal experience can be described as a path of self-development that is concerned with awakening the individual seeker to the real nature of existence. Seekers intuitively recognize that there is more to life than the daily round and our mundane pastimes and preoccupations, however much we may be attached to these experiences.

Generally, we look outside ourselves for fulfilment and it is easy to get

caught up with striving to achieve some goal that lies just out of reach. Contemporary society conditions us to believe that material objects, hedonistic pursuits or success in the world can bring us happiness. Yet our subjective experiences show us that nothing external can really meet the need for deeper engagement and an experience of connection and completeness.

Meditation – one way of preparing the individual for awakening him- or herself to the true nature of existence.

This statue of the Buddha, commissioned by the emperor Ashoka, 3rd century BCE, sits before the Great Stupa, Sanchi, India.

A seeker is someone with a sense of longing for something more. According to Gnostic scholar Peter Kingsley, when you want what's so much greater than yourself, there's no chance of feeling fulfilled by transient rewards. And Gnostic teachings insist that once you refuse to settle for anything less, the experience of fullness comes to you. Kingsley describes it rather poetically: 'People who love the divine go around with holes in their hearts, and inside the hole is the universe'. In the eastern tradition, those on the spiritual path are usually guided by an experienced teacher, or guru, who prescribes practices such as meditation that prepare the individual for awakening.

Consciousness and the path to non-duality

Many species have a mind, but may not be conscious in the sense that we humans are. Being conscious is a mental quality that gives us the awareness that we exist and a sense of what existence might mean. We usually experience ourselves, our thoughts and feelings as separate from the rest of reality – but the truth is, this view is what ultimately separates us from reality. For the physicist Einstein, our own limited consciousness is what imprisons us in a narrow world. He argued that a substantially new manner of thinking is crucial if humanity is to survive the serious threats to the survival of our species that we face today. That thinking is often defined as non-duality – meaning that there is no separation between self and other, or self and the rest of the world.

Enlightenment

On the spiritual path, Easterners refer to dissolving the sense of self into what might be called universal consciousness – that which pervades everything, from the point of view of metaphysics and quantum mechanics. Progress on the spiritual path is measured by the degree to which the self is liberated from the prison of materialism – the belief that we are matter, and that matter and spirit are divided. The goal of liberation from the self is called enlightenment or self-realization. The process is one of understanding the real nature of existence – non-duality – and this knowledge deeply transforms your lived experience.

Mudras are sacred hand positions, used to seal energy flows during meditation. This statue uses Gyan Mudra to indicate meditative awareness and the icon may represent an energy centre or a deity.

'Awakening' (samadhi) implies waking up to your true nature. 'Enlightened' teachers say that this is how we are, and always have been – it's just that we are so busily immersed in the daily round that we don't notice that existence is not about doing, but about being. In spite of all this preparation, awakening is considered to arise spontaneously – it's one of those states that tend to recede the more you strive after it.

Awakening to bliss

People who have experienced bliss have a more integrated understanding of the nature of reality – of feeling connected in a universe that is also a multiverse, in which each of us is linked to the myriad aspects of life. Awakening is variously described as conscious awareness, liberation, spaciousness of mind, oneness and bliss. Philosopher Ken Wilber describes it as Big Mind, while we normally inhabit Small Mind. People who have glimpsed the transcendent nature of this reality describe it as a complete acceptance of how things are, rather than any kind of euphoria.

The language may vary, but we can get a sense of the qualities of experience that mystics are talking about.

The bliss that is a transcendental goal belongs to an entirely different order of existence from an orgasmic feeling or sensation. It describes the state of 'being-ness', when all feelings, sensations and thoughts have become totally irrelevant. It is hard to find the words to describe this –

The seven chakras associated with tantric meditation are illuminated on the Buddha.

Hinduism and Buddhism are full of complex terms, all of which have specific meanings and semantic, cultural and metaphysical associations honed over millennia. But words get in the way of the actual experience. As Tantric scholar Georg Feuerstein describes it:

> *In the ecstatic condition of identity with Being, the body stands revealed as the universe itself. The physical frame is found to be not solid, after all, but a vast ocean of energy in which all bodies are interconnected. This is the great oneness taught about by tantric adepts. Bliss is the everlasting 'orgasm' of God and Goddess in divine embrace, beyond all concepts.*

Dr Deepak Chopra quotes Nisargadatta Maharaj's perspective (from *I Am That*):

> *Bliss is my very nature*
> *I need not do anything nor strive for anything to secure it.*
> *Bliss follows me wherever I go*
> *It is more real to me than my body,*
> *It is nearer to me than my mind.*
> *Happiness that is dependent on something is*
> *only another form of misery.*

Meditating together can bring great rewards for your relationship – deepening intimacy.

According to those who have reached this rarefied state, bliss is not something that you can make happen by following a formula or by grasping at passing tastes of ecstasy. Bliss arises spontaneously, even if spiritual teachers maintain that it is already part of your being and simply requires a profound change of perspective in order for you to realize this. Mystics say that it always comes unsought, provided you prepare for it – rather like insight, which most often comes when you are not worrying at a particular problem. Instead, it may come when you are in the flow of doing something else, swimming, or walking – but not ruminating.

Rituals and meditation prepare you for spiritual awakening by clearing your mind of the endless chatter of daily thoughts and by opening your senses, so that bodily awareness creates another layer of engagement. Such practices provide a spiritual discipline aimed at enabling you to receive an experience of the timeless nature of bliss. Common spiritual practices include breath work, visualization of the body's subtle anatomy or energy system and the flow of energies (see page 194), and practices to stimulate your serpent power (see page 200).

Dharma and Karma

An ethical framework for daily life is considered fundamental for aspirants on the spiritual path. Dharma refers to the sustaining principles that uphold a harmonious sense of order; it encompasses the need to protect, care for and serve others.

Dharma is allied to an understanding of karma, in which inconsiderate or wrong action has harmful consequences. The closest idea that we are familiar with is that what goes around comes around – the consequences of our actions catch up with us eventually. The key idea is the need to develop conscious awareness about the actions that you take.

The Dharma-chakra or wheel of law has been represented as a chariot wheel since the time of the Buddhist king Ashoka.

Yoga and the spiritual path

Yoga is a traditional Hindu approach to the union of body, mind and spirit. Literally meaning 'yoke' or unification, it involves integrating body, mind and soul in the purpose of ultimate freedom. Ultimately the goal is that one becomes free of the chains of cause and effect (karma) that lock humans into the endless cycle of reincarnations. Hindus and Buddhists believe in reincarnation in the form of any sentient being. One of the broader aims of the spiritual path is to get off this endless wheel of incarnation.

Simply being

Most of us are overly focused on what we are doing, rather than on simply being. We are caught up in action rather than awareness. It is hard to even imagine a state of complete calmness and repose in which thoughts and emotions cease to dance in perpetual motion – yet it is through stillness and tranquillity that we are more likely to achieve a level of personal

equanimity, to use the Buddhist term. Traditions from the Bible to yoga recommend that we 'Be still and know God'. Meditation and yoga offer techniques for stilling our turbulent thoughts and restless bodies, which prevent us from knowing ourselves as part of the spaciousness of the divine.

Ordinarily our awareness and energies are directed outward, to material objects, hedonistic pastimes and worldly success. Yoga is a

simple process of reversing the outward flow of energy and consciousness so that the mind turns inward. The mind and body become one integrated whole – a dynamic centre of direct perception that no longer depends on us interpreting events through our senses but is capable of experiencing truth directly.

Living in constant awareness of spirituality is referred to as enlightenment – the goal of all forms of yoga and other spiritual practices.

Daily yoga and meditation introduce us to a different experience of reality, and are key practices in Asian spiritual methods. There are many different styles of yoga – some include hand gestures (mudra) to meditate.

Steps on the yogic path

In the *Yoga Sutras*, Patanjali (who lived in India around the start of the Christian era) sets out eight 'limbs' or steps to freedom on the yogic path – to quieting one's mind and achieving kaivalya, or total detachment. The Sutras were the first text to record and systematize the yoga traditions that were around in Patanjali's lifetime. The division into the Eight Limbs is reminiscent of Buddha's Noble Eightfold Path.

1 Following the precepts of ethical living: honesty,
   forgiveness and non-violence.
2 Cultivating calm and contentment.
3 Balancing basic posture.
4 Practice of breath control (pranayama).
5 The mind is focused inward and developed.
6 Practice of focusing.
7 Practice of meditation.
8 Samadhi – dissolution of the self into a unified field of consciousness.

Meditation reveals that it is our ignorance that results in the separation of subject and object – and our own experience of splitting, opposition and conflict. Through meditation the accumulations of tension, anxiety and inflexible thinking, which bind, knot and restrict us, are released without effort.

This Korean painting of the life of the Buddha, in Jogyesa, shows how even as a child lotus flowers – symbols of enlightenment supposedly bloomed under his feet.

Mirabai

Mirabai (c.1498–1550), a Rajastani princess, became enraptured by Lord Krishna, hero of the Bhagavad Gita (a Hindu sacred text that translates as The Song of God) and one of the manifestations of the god Vishnu at an

This painting shows Lord Krishna awakening kundalini with his flute, and dates from the 17th century.

early age. After her husband's death she became a wandering mystic, devoting her life to singing Krishna's praises. She considered herself a reincarnation of Lalita, who was mad with love for Krishna.

Mirabai's poetry is about freedom, breaking with tradition and trusting completely in the divine. Her devotional songs illustrated a high point in the bhakti renaissance. Her erotic poetry expresses her complete surrender to longing, and her madness in love. Krishna has dominion over snakes, and Krishna-varna refers to a dark snake, as described in the poem below:

In All My Lives

In all my lives you have been with me;
whether day or night I remember.
When you fall out of my sight, I am restless
day and night, burning.
I climb hilltops; I watch for signs of your return;
my eyes are swollen with tears.
The ocean of life – that's not genuine, the ties
of family, the obligations to the world –
they're not genuine.
It is your beauty that makes me drunk.

From *Mirabai: Ecstatic Poems*, translation:
Robert Bly and Jane Hirshfield

Forms of yoga

According to the Hindu text *Bhagavid Gita* there are four main paths to spiritual realization: those of knowledge, mastery of mind, devotion and service. However, there are probably as many different paths as there are people! A number of established paths have evolved, including:

Hatha yoga (the yoga of body posture)

Hatha means sun and moon. This path is about integrating opposites through care of the body and breathing techniques and has been popular in the West for decades. There are also complementary elements that can be described as solar/lunar, masculine/feminine, and so on, which are harmonized by balancing the body through posture and exercises (asanas). Breathing exercises (pranayama) are used to direct the breath throughout the body, calming, centring and balancing it.

Bhakti yoga (the yoga of devotion)

In the path of love and devotion, the emphasis is on developing an attitude of love towards others. The adepts channel their feelings of devotion into worship of the deities and service to others.

Jnana yoga (the path of knowledge)

Through discriminating thought and deeper understanding, one steps out of ignorant ways of conducting life and cultivates a deeper knowledge of the true nature of reality. Energy follows awareness, so it is important to purify your mind and clarify your intentions.

Mosaic depicting the sound of the universe – the sacred mantra 'Om'.

Tibetan Buddhists believe repeating the prayer 'Om Mani Pad Me Hum',
invokes the blessings of Chenrezig, the embodiment of compassion. It is
often carved in stone, placed on shrines or by the side of the pathway.

Karma yoga (the path of action)

Through right living and selfless service to others and the community, one
learns to dissolve negative karma and break the chain of cause and effect.

Raja yoga (the path of power)

The path of mastering oneself. Through mediation one develops mental
control and sometimes special powers.

Kriya yoga (the path of awareness)

Awareness permeates mind, ideas and actions, so that one functions in harmony. Yogananda, one of its adherents, is believed to have chosen the time of his death and transited harmoniously.

Laya yoga (the path of absorption)

Dissolving the small self into the energy of the divine leads to an experience of reality as bliss. The method involves absorbing cosmic principles to become one with the luminous quality of consciousness.

Kundalini yoga (the path of awakening the serpent)

Meditation rituals focus on awakening the root energy or fire and channelling this through the subtle energy centres (chakras) up the body by means of yoga postures and breath control. Once the energy climbs to the crown of the head, enlightened awareness opens and flowers like a thousand-petalled lotus blossom.

Tantra yoga (the path of bliss)

Through weaving kundalini yoga together with 'left-handed practices' such as eating meat, drinking alcohol and ritual sex, one takes the fast path to dissolving the ego and living out the Tantric reality – that the whole universe is a manifestation of masculine and feminine principles united in blissful harmony.

Mantra yoga (the yoga of sound)

This focuses the energy of sound on transformation, and involves the chanting of sacred phrases (mantras). Recitations are believed to tune the body to certain energetic frequencies. Transcendental meditation is a popular application of this in the West.

Exercise: Mantra meditation on the word for mother

The primal power of a name

In mantra meditation you focus on the sound you are making, and attune yourself to its resonance. Hindu meditators attune to the sound waves of the universe by making resonant sounds that fill the throat, chest and head with vibrations. Keep your lips closed, relax your jaw and throat, and hum: you will feel the resonance filling your throat and chest. Experienced mediators use this kind of practice to plug in to an experience of life as pure energy.

1 Sit relaxed and allow your breathing to slow and deepen, as you breathe in peace and stillness, and breathe out tension or worries. Breathe deeply for a few minutes. As you breathe out, repeat 'Ma'. If you prefer, you can switch to humming Mmm. Keep your throat and jaw relaxed to allow the sound to vibrate in the area.

2 Chant for several minutes, feeling the sound resonate in your body and mind. As you chant you can imagine the loving feelings that arise from your connection with your mother, and let them expand through your body. Your mother's love for you as a baby is a conduit for the all-embracing love of the divine mother. Don't get distracted by thoughts about whether she loved you or not, or whether there is a divine mother. Just invoke feelings of love, and allow them to permeate, and radiate through you and out into the world, as you become a channel for unconditional love.

3 As you continue saying the mantra Ma, or just humming Mmmmm ... with a relaxed throat, send out waves of love with the sound. If you get distracted, go back to repeating the sound and allow yourself to get absorbed in the sensory pleasure of your vibrating body and the quality of the sound.

Ma, the Bliss Mother

The Hindu saint Anandamayi Ma (1896–1982) was known as the 'bliss-permeated mother', or more familiarly as 'mother'. Her followers called her simply 'Ma', or 'mother', as she radiated unconditional love.

She was not a formal teacher (guru), but expressed her experience of the sublime through advice based on her own experience of absorption in the divine – a state of ecstasy:

Cherish the company of those who are helpful to your quest, avoid those who distract you. In other words, hold fast to the Good and shun the merely pleasurable. If you live in this spirit, the help you need will come to you naturally.

For Ma, her essence was timeless and unchanging – its form and gender were incidental to her spiritual nature. A Tantric, she taught people to follow their own calling, including women.

She broke tradition in 1936 by initiating her women disciples with the Gayatri mantra (referring to the supreme being as 'he'), which had been closed to women for centuries, despite its provenance as a great Shakti mantra – an invocation to the goddess Shakti, which was believed to increase shakti energy through reciting the prayer. The guru Swami Vivekananda translated the mantra as: 'We meditate on the glory of that Being who has produced this universe; may He enlighten our minds.'

Virgin in the prayer pose with hands together. This is similar to the 'namaste' greeting and is common to many religions.

Chakras and the subtle energy system

Yoga practitioners have developed a system in which they map a series of energy centres and conduits for linking this energy through the body. Chakra literally means 'wheel', and chakras are conceptualized as whorls or vortices of energy clustered in particular areas. There are many maps of energy centres, but in this book we are using the accepted system of seven main ones positioned from the base of the spine to the top of the head, in the area that we would call the central nervous system (spine and brain). The energy clusters inside the body correlate to energy

The main seven chakras (left) and their correlates (opposite). Each chakra is associated with a mantra, a colour, and deities, and they are crucial to tantric traditions.

constellations outside the body and can also be represented by sounds, geometric images (yantras) or deities. Yoga teachers have developed exercises to master or harness these energies for self-development. During visualization, practitioners imagine the energy moving into the areas to which they want to direct it. Little packages of consciousness called seeds, or drops, flow along pathways and are charged either 'positive' or 'negative'. Concentrating on these intensifies your energy.

CHAKRA	CORRELATES
Sex centre	Male positive pole, red, survival, sexuality, instinct, grounding
Lower belly	Female positive pole, orange, emotions, birth and death
Solar plexus	Male positive pole, yellow, the seat of one's unique journey
Heart	Female positive pole, green, love, nurturing, compassion, bridge between body and mind
Throat	Male positive pole, turquoise, creativity, self-realization
Centre of brain (level with centre of eyebrows)	Female positive pole, blue, intuition, communion
Crown of head	Beyond duality, violet, consciousness

Chakras and sexual evolution

The chakra system is a map for spiritual development that reminds us that every change in consciousness has a corresponding change in energy, or sexuality, in the body. The current new-age chakra map is based on the traditional description of each chakra and its associations, which is as follows:

Level One	**Root** – the energy of food and nourishment
Level Two	**Navel** – the energy of sex (when it is not harnessed in service of the sacred)
Level Three	**Solar plexus** – the energy of power or intentionality
Level Four	**Heart** – the energy of love
Level Five	**Throat** – the energy of self-expression or self-actualization
Level Six	**Brow** – the energy of self-transcendence
Level Seven	**Crown** – the energy of oneness with the All

Each level of consciousness represents an increase in care, compassion, love, concern and awareness. Every stage of consciousness is supported by its own quality of energy, or prana. Prana means vital energy – like many spiritual traditions, it also implies 'breath', which is responsible for uniting different chakras within the body and one organism to another as well as for uniting one organism with the entire universe.

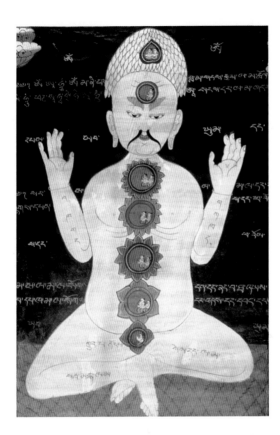

This page from a popular Hindu text depicts the seven chakras quite clearly as flowers with a number of petals.

This non-dual experience of oneness is what the great liberation from normal reality is all about. It brings you a deliverance from the limitations of the small self and the small self's experience of sexuality. This model provides a framework for understanding how sexuality evolves in the same way that consciousness does.

A chakra visualization

Go with the flow

In this exercise, focus on drawing the energy from the base of your spine, up the inner flute towards the top of the head, energizing the chakras along the way. Breathe deeply and slowly, imagining energy moving with the flow of your breathing. Such exercises form the basis of Tantric techniques and are even incorporated into more advanced techniques.

1 Choose a posture that you feel comfortable with. Then relax the body by concentrating on each part in turn, allowing the stress in that area to fall away.

2 Now focus on your breathing, allowing it to become deeper and more regular, without force. If your mind wanders, gently bring it back to an awareness of each breath you take. Feel the energy of each breath sustaining you.

3 Try to visualize energy entering your body with each breath, whether in the form of light or some other quality. Imagine a channel down the centre of your body, from your mouth to your genitals. As you breathe in, imagine you are drawing energy in through your mouth and down this inner flute to the base of your spine. As you breathe out, imagine that the energy is flowing back up the inner flute to be released out of your mouth.

4 Spend several minutes enjoying the in-and-out flow of your breath, relaxing yet allowing the subtle energy to invigorate you.

5 With every out breath, imagine the energy flowing up and by-passing your mouth, going to the top of your head.

6 As you breathe in, let the energy flow down to your sexual area, and with every out breath, let the energy flow upwards and stream out of the top of your head.

7 After several minutes, open your eyes and slowly come back to your normal awareness.

Kundalini yoga

Practitioners call Kundalini yoga 'the yoga of awareness', because they claim it increases self-knowledge and unleashes the creative potential that exists within every human being. In kundalini yoga, meditation focuses on awakening the serpent power believed to lie dormant in the root chakra, or generative centre. Once awake, this energy is raised through the successive chakras, stimulating them, until it ultimately climbs to the top of the head.

Once it gathers here it leads to altered states of consciousness that are described as bliss (see page 176) leading to realization (nirvana), where the adept remains awakened. In the language of the yogis, the goal of kundalini yoga is to awaken the cosmic energy of kundalini and unite it with Shiva, described as the pure consciousness pervading the whole universe.

This Indian minature c. 1850 shows the primal Kundalini being awakened and refined through the seven energy centres, and ultimately flowering in bliss, represented by sacred sex.

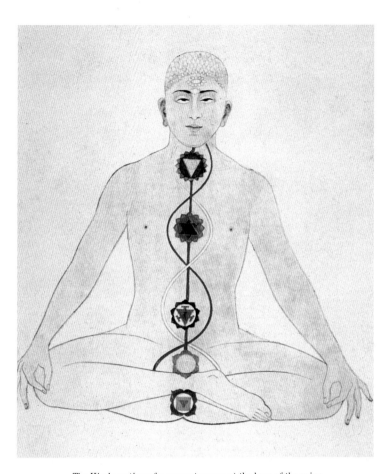

The Hindu notion of a serpent power at the base of the spine
approximates to Freud's idea of libido, characterized by him both as
life energy and also as a sexual imperative – as we acknowledge
when we use the word libido to refer to our sex drive.

Kundalini meditation

Awareness of anatomy

Kundalini meditations use the breath and visualization to awaken the dynamic serpent power and unite it with conscious awareness. Yogic meditations such as this help you to balance your breath (prana), develop concentration – and also help your ability to visualize. Many people are visual and find that imagining the colours traditionally associated with the chakras helps them to meditate. Some use sound – there are different mantras associated with each chakra.

This particular meditation is aimed at developing your awareness of the subtle anatomy of the body and the kundalini, latent libidinal energy. In the exercise you spend 10 or 15 minutes drawing light up through the channel thought to be located up the spine, successively animating each of the seven chakra energy wheels mapped onto the body.

1 Sit comfortably with your legs crossed. If you cannot sit with your legs crossed, a chair is fine. Sit with your spine straight, relax your stomach and close your eyes. Bring your attention to your breath and allow it naturally to slow down, for a few minutes.

2 Now bring your awareness to the base of your spine and imagine yourself breathing from there, rather than from your lungs. As you inhale and exhale, visualize the breath coming into and leaving the area around your genitals and anus. Continue for a few minutes until that area feels alive.

3 Picture a small ball of energy forming at the base of your spine, getting stronger until it radiates a warm red colour.

4 Imagine this ball moving up the spine, becoming orange as it moves to the level of your navel. With every in-breath, allow the orange colour to spread through your navel, as you feel more calm and comfortable.

5 When you are ready, encourage the orange ball to spread upwards into your solar plexus, just below the centre of your ribcage, where it becomes yellowish, radiating light and energy like a sun. With every in-breath, allow this sun to warm and relax your whole body.

6 When the energy moves up to the area of your heart – between your breasts – imagine the colour becoming the vibrant green of plant growth, nature and nurture. Allow your heart to feel nourished and radiate loving feelings throughout your being.

7 In the area of your throat the light becomes turquoise, animating your throat area with an ethereal violet colour. After some minutes, imagine the coloured ball climbing towards your forehead with every in-breath.

8 In the middle of your forehead, in the area commonly known as your third eye, the energy wheel becomes indigo blue. This is the colour associated with mystery and the threshold between the physical and psychic worlds.

9 Finally, the energy rises to the top of your head where it unfolds into a many-coloured rainbow, in which light and energy flow up through your nervous system and out into the world around you. Let the energy flow through your whole chakra system to the top of your head, where its abundance merges with the energy of the cosmos. Stay with this meditation until you find yourself coming back to earth.

Sacred knowledge

The practice of yoga is linked to Hinduism, under whose broad umbrella are gathered many local and diverse traditions. Formal Hinduism, that is associated with its texts, is usually referred to as Vedic Hinduism. The source of the Hindu Vedas was drawn from the rich oral traditions of early Indus civilizations, and gathered into texts in Sanskrit around 3000 BCE. The word 'Veda' comes from the Sanskrit vid, meaning 'knowledge' – the Vedas are 'sacred knowledge'. Their exact date is controversial, but India is widely considered home to the longest continuous civilization on earth. Its sophisticated spiritual traditions have profoundly influenced contemporary religion and philosophy, drawing on cultural knowledge that may date back to 10,000 years BCE.

The basic collections of texts include the Vedas, Upanishads, the *Bhagavad Gita* and the *Brahma Sutra*. While the bustling pantheon

of gods and goddesses within Hinduism may lead the casual onlooker to assume that they are all different, texts repeatedly stress the fact that the different goddesses and gods are merely different aspects of the same

3rd century relief which shows the death of the Buddha or the last stage of his enlightenment; final liberation from the cycle of rebirth, or Parinirvana.

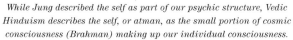

*While Jung described the self as part of our psychic structure, Vedic
Hinduism describes the self, or atman, as the small portion of cosmic
consciousness (Brahman) making up our individual consciousness.*

goddess. Just as individual humans are all unique reflections of life, so
the different gods and goddesses are different manifestations of the
one creation. The Vedas and the Upanishads, which explored Hindu
philosophy, describe reality as a single, unified, changeless and eternal
Brahman (God). The ordinary human world of separate objects is an
illusion. Through meditation, each person can experience his or her own
Self as inseparable from the One. This is the meaning of 'enlightenment' –
to realize that you are the same as the divine reality.

Meditation as a route to enlightenment

Allied to breath and energy work of various strands of yoga is the practice of meditation. Meditation is key to developing a calm and grounded internal state, as a basis for practices that can alter your perception and experience of reality. It is a practical technique through which individuals can access some of the rarefied states referred to by seers and mystics throughout the ages. Both Hindu and Buddhist approaches to enlightenment rely on the use of meditation, often allied with visualization.

The first step in meditation is to learn to screen out external stimuli, such as noise and other sensory manifestations but also thoughts and emotions. In meditation you realize that these are background distractions, just like noise, and that there is a different way of experiencing yourself. Different styles of meditation direct your attention to your breath or sound, or harness your mind in ritual practice or visualization.

Being rather than doing

Visualizations harness the powerful resources of the imagination to change your attitudes. In order to engage all the senses, meditation includes music, visual mandalas, physical mudras (hand gestures) and postures, so it can involve total immersion. The aim of meditation is not to take you somewhere else, but to enable you to get rid of the mental

Meditation – going inward – is a basis for all spiritual practices, and includes many techniques to alter your perception of reality.

clutter and sensory distractions that assail us, and uncover a fundamental simplicity – pure existence. Buddhists such as James Low, author of *Simply Being*, describe our fundamental nature as a state of unchanging innate purity, which is at the heart of everything we do and is who we really are. Whereas Christian cosmology describes the fundamental nature of man as tainted by original sin, in Dzogchen Buddhism, simply 'being' refers to dwelling in our natural perfection.

Words are an imperfect medium to describe intangible states that we can only access through experience and a state that is, by its nature, wordless. That is probably why esoteric traditions have developed lengthy and complex discourses in an attempt to describe something that, at the same time, masters describe as recovering an innate simplicity. Meditation is not an abstract idea, but involves allowing the vital energy that animates us to emerge. Buddhist teaching recalls us to the open nature of all things, the natural state we have never left, yet have somehow forgotten. Maybe another way of describing it is as 'openness' – being open to experience.

This is a more colloquial comment by film-maker David Lynch, who says:

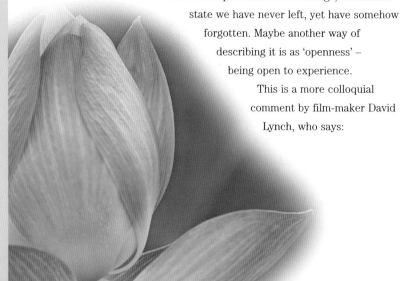

'... [meditation] takes you to an ocean of pure consciousness, pure knowingness. But it's familiar; it's you. And right away a sense of happiness emerges – not a goofball happiness, but a thick beauty.' (The word 'thick' was coined by anthropologist Richard Geertz to describe rich and multilayered experiences.)

French Buddhist Matthieu Ricard, described by some as the happiest man in the world, puts his contentment down to meditation. Scientists searching for material evidence of the elusive quality of happiness have studied his brain functioning exhaustively.

Retrain your brain

Neurobiological research suggests that meditation produces a permanent restructuring of the brain. In the brains of long-term Buddhist meditators, who typically spend many hours dwelling on unconditional loving-kindness and compassion, the brain produces different kinds of waves to the rest of us. These waves were associated with meditators' advanced abilities to cultivate positive emotions, emotional stability and mindful behaviour. Other studies amply demonstrate that you don't have to be a yogi to reap the benefits of meditation. Even those who participate in short-term training courses can alter their brains. Researchers showed that changes were most dramatic in the area of the brain involved in emotion regulation.

Hindus agree with this strategy for achieving equanimity. In the *Yoga Sutras*, Patanjali described how to cultivate a calm and equitable nature: 'Undisturbed calmness of mind is attained by cultivating friendliness toward the happy, compassion for the unhappy, delight in the virtuous, and indifference toward the wicked.'

Mindfulness as meditation

Mindfulness is often spoken of as the heart of Buddhist meditation. For beginners the breath is the major focus of awareness, and is later integrated with a range of different experiences. Mindfulness can incorporate breathing with emotional waves as they rise up, and also sounds and thoughts – and interruptions – anything that arises. If thoughts keep interfering with your focus, move your attention to your emotions or physical sensations, in order to stop getting hooked on the content of your thoughts. Most people have to cultivate awareness in their own bodies, and for the people in their own lives, before going on to develop empathy and compassion for the people around them. The techniques are secondary to the cultivation of a clear mind and compassionate heart.

To attain a certain clarity of mind, it's a good idea to start with developing calmness. Mindfulness is a meditation style that has been developed for a Western setting by psychologist Jon Kabat-Zinn, who drew from Zen Buddhism, hatha yoga and other disciplines to create an accessible form called mindfulness-based stress reduction. Available in health service settings it is practised by many therapists in the West.

Back to basics

While teaching very basic techniques such as watching the breath, Kabat-Zinn also reminds us that mindfulness is about cultivating calmness, concentration and clear perception, in which one develops inner wisdom in the context of right living and right thinking – which are fundamental

One of 72 Buddhas, this 8th century shrine at Borobudur Temple, Yogyakarta, Java, Indonesia directs pilgrims to pass through the world of desires, and forms and into the world of formlessness.

Buddhist precepts. The end goal of Buddhism is enlightenment, where any notion of a separate self falls away from your essence. Mindfulness is also one of the basic methods of focusing our awareness on the spaciousness underlying our thoughts. In meditation you simply witness your thoughts, without getting attached to the content of those thoughts.

Buddhism

Buddhists believe that there is no thinker behind the thought and that thought is merely the way the energy of our mind makes itself known. We make a mistake when we imagine that our thoughts say anything about who we are. According to Sri Lankan Buddhist, Professor Walpola Rahula, the Buddhist view is totally opposed to the Western world view that we

inherited from Descartes and the famous saying, 'I think, therefore I am.'

Becoming a Buddhist isn't necessarily about embracing metaphysics, although it appeals to Western atheistic intellectuals. It can be a matter of following the dharma (teaching), and joining the Buddhist community (the sangha) as Christians join the church.

18th-century diagram of the Buddhist world mountain as a mandala. 31 layers of existence rise to a peak in the heavens. A further 18 levels ascend to a higher heaven (top).

*In the Himalayan mountains Buddhist prayer flags send blessings
through the world. Originating from the pre-Buddhist Bon practices of Tibet,
the message of the Sutras or sacred texts is also transmitted through banners.*

The Buddhist path

Buddha taught that suffering is everywhere, and it is caused by desire or
attachment, and that negative emotions such as anger or indifference get
in the way of enlightenment. The Buddhist path prescribes a moral code
involving right attitude, thought, speech and conduct. Developing right
focus and effort involves cultivating mindfulness, reflection, equanimity in
the face of conflict and challenges and joyfulnesses.

To cultivate these qualities, the most essential thing is your intention
– since actions follow thoughts. Regular practice is often needed to
develop the capacity to extend love and compassion to all living beings
without reservation.

Emptiness

In the Zen Buddhist tradition there is only energy. This energy is that of existence itself, which Buddhists describe as emptiness. This emptiness may be full of stuff – the world we see around us and all its phenomena – but the phenomena are full of spaciousness, just as we know from quantum mechanics. This is what is meant by the famous Zen Buddhist saying, 'Form is emptiness, and emptiness is form.'

In Buddhism, the intention is that we become aware of the emptiness underneath all the drama of our lives, in order to help us detach from thoughts, emotions, our occupation and preoccupations, from everything

that causes us misery, pain or suffering. Meditation is the key means of bringing about this change, and Buddhist mediations can take many forms (see the section on Mindfulness, page 212).

The Bhava-chakra (wheel of karma) warns of the dangers of samsara (being caught in illusion about the reality of existence). Getting off the cycle of endless reincarnation is a goal of meditation.

This delicate temple statue in Cambodia connects the navel
with the heart centre – the chakra between the breasts.

Exercise: Dissolving the ego

Reflect on nothing

Buddhists tend to use reflection or mental enquiry as a way into a meditative state of mind. Use this reflective exercise to consider how much your identity changes during the course of your life, depending on your upbringing, environment and the experiences you accumulate.

Once you realize that you are fundamentally empty, you can let go of a fixed world view. Letting go of any limiting beliefs that you may hold is necessary in order for you to begin to fulfil your potential. The ego is made up of all the aspects that we habitually consider make up our identity – our thoughts, our character, our job, our social roles – but these are only the external trappings; if you can clear your mind of all these things, you are on the way to being able to achieve a state of bliss.

Spend a few moments looking at how you are not any of the things you normally describe yourself as – you are not your gender, your mood, your illness, your ambitions:

1 I am not my job. My occupation changes depending on my circumstances.
2 I am not defined by my relationships with partner, children or family.
3 I am not my race or gender. All humans are fundamentally the same.
4 I am not my body. My body will age, and suffer illness, but my awareness is bigger than my bodily experience.
5 I am not my mind. Thoughts come and go.
6 I am not my emotions. Feelings pass.
7 I am not my past. There is only the eternal present.
8 I am not my physical form. I am a form of energy.

Sacred sex and Buddhism

Sacred sex is seen as a gateway through which you can step into an immediate meeting with the divine. It is a doorway that uses our body, energy, emotions and mind to step into a dimension that is more than the sum of these things. However, while Hinduism, with its body-positive practices of yoga and strong devotional ethos, is wide enough to encompass sexual practices in the service of the sacred, sacred sex seems to be altogether less visceral in the Buddhist tradition.

In Buddhism, sacred sex is considered a very sophisticated practice, which requires years of preparation. We see sex as a means of gratification, yet spiritual practitioners see it as a force that can threaten our hard-won peace of mind. The work in Buddhism, as in so many spiritual traditions, is to harmonize our Small Mind into Big Mind, or consciousness. The purpose of Buddhism is to understand the true nature of reality and offer the means to do so: through self-development. The goal is enlightenment – a state in which one profoundly understands reality and lives it. The path is through cultivating compassion, wisdom and understanding. From this perspective, any meeting with another is like meeting ourselves – or the universal and transcendent essence of ourselves. The meeting of two beings involves a dance of energy. This is because, according to Buddha (the enlightened being, Shakyamuni, who lived in North India around 500 BCE), the world is in continuous flux and is impermanent; therefore people and objects are insubstantial forms within which energy ceaselessly moves. There is no god-like figure or unmoving mover behind the movement. Life and movement are one.

*This Tibetan thangka, shows Shakyamuni Buddha with
a host of Buddhas (enlightened beings).*

Tantra Deities

and Practices

Tantra, the way of connection

Tantra is an esoteric tradition within both Hinduism and Buddhism.
A dynamic, living tradition, Tantra refers to the interwovenness of
things, actions and events. Tantras are also the texts used by these
marginal groups. Tantra traces its roots to the pre-Vedic Dravidian
practices of the Indus Valley millennia ago, and these practices are deeply
embedded within Hinduism; this in turn influenced Tibetan Buddhism.
Just as Tibetan Buddhism (which developed from Buddhism in India)
incorporated elements of the earlier Bon religion, so Hinduism appears to
retain many practices and beliefs that are of great antiquity. Bon had a lot

*Close-up of a ritual hand gesture. This is the mudra for teaching
from the heart, where the right hand represents method, while the left
hand represents wisdom.*

of shamanic practices and was concerned with mediating man's relation with nature and the elements, while Tantra derives from mother and goddess worship. This explains its more body-positive and visceral aspects, as well as the central motif of sacred sex – the divine couple and their blissful union. Sexual union is seen as cosmogonic – endlessly creating and sustaining the world. Just as the sexual union of Shakti and Shiva is considered necessary to sustain creation, so, too, are the ritual sex practices of their devotees.

Hindu and Buddhist Tantra have followed different trajectories in the last couple of millennia. Whereas a Buddhist approach rests on cultivating an attitude of peaceable equanimity, a key technique of Hindu Tantric meditation practices appears to involve stimulating desires and passions in order to drive personal transformation.

Due to the Tibetan diaspora after Chinese occupation, Tibetan Buddhism has been widely disseminated in the West, and the combination of intellectualism and the practice of meditation very much appeals to educated Western seekers. Tantra in India is much less well understood, despite the fact that it underpins Tibetan Buddhism; it remains a largely oral tradition that is popular among the lower castes.

Tantra is part of the perennial philosophy we explored earlier in relation to alchemy (see page 62), which sees the body as containing and representing all the forces of the universe. On a metaphysical level this means that practitioners treat the universe as if it were within us, and ourselves as if we were the universe. Further, the forces governing the cosmos on the macro-level are believed to govern the individual on the micro-level. According to Tantra, the individual being and universe are one – thus all that exists in the universe also exists in the individual body.

Non-conformists

Like Gnosticism, Tantra constitutes a multitude of non-conformist theories and practices, with teachers and different sects interpreting apocryphal teachings and texts in their own ways. Gnostics were treated as heretics because their founding beliefs were often at odds with those of the Church, which steadily acquired more and more control over the material lives of Christians. As we know from the inglorious Inquisition, the Church believed it was the custodian of our immortal souls, and it was therefore justified in doing away with the bodies of those souls they pronounced to be in immortal danger.

Hinduism has never been anywhere near as hegemonic as Catholicism, and by and large the fate of the soul is felt to be something that is within the personal scope of the individual to develop. There is a notion of perfectibility, in that enlightenment releases humans from mortal cares and consequences, yet there isn't the same notion of being damned as a result of one's imperfections that once drove much of the Christian and Judaic traditions.

The left-hand path

Tantra adheres to the Hindu notion of reality as being unified rather than non-dual, but acknowledges the conjunction of complementary forces. Opposing forces – whether of heaven and earth, woman and man, being and doing – are all united and differences are dissolved in such a way that the underlying unity of everything is revealed. Tantra emphasizes first-hand exploration and experience, rather than blindly following custom

*Flamboyantly interlocked maithuna, or lovemaking couple, depicted
in relief on the eternal walls at the Khajuraho temples
(built c.950 to 1150), India.*

and tradition. In fact, it considers such methods inferior and often
delights in espousing radically different opinions. Tantric practices are
considered by their gurus to offer a fast track for spiritual seekers during
our materialistic age, known as the Age of Kali. Tantra is often described
as the 'left-hand path', because it uses practices customarily forbidden to
higher-caste Hindus, the Brahmins (the left hand being considered
unclean in India). The main transgressive practices are the five Ms:
madya (liquor), mamsa (meat), matsya (fish), mudra (grain) and

maithuna (sexual intercourse – it has long been Tantrics' custom to worship the Hindu goddess Shakti, the Divine Goddess, by seeking unity of body and soul in communal sex rites). Ritual intercourse in Tantra can be seen in the same spirit as the confrontation of personal and cultural taboos about death by ritual practice in cremation grounds. In India, if not burnt, some bodies are left exposed in the cremation ground to be

Reading the Texts

The *Kularnava Tantra* is the major Tantra of the Kula School in north India, which influenced almost all later Tantric works. The title translates as something like 'Ocean of the Mother's Family' and was recorded around 1150 CE and translated by Sri M.P. Pandit and Arthur Avalon (also known as Sir John Woodroffe) in 1916.

In common with all esoteric traditions, its ambiguous language describes teachings and rituals in metaphors designed to keep the actual practices secret. According to Mike Magee, a Sanskrit scholar who has done a huge amount of rigorous research on Tantra, everything has a gross, a subtle and a supreme meaning and may refer to either methods or metaphoric meanings.

While many terms can be taken at face value, a literal meaning is not always intended, although at times the multiple meanings refer to the multiple layers of meaning inherent in ritual practices. For instance, a cremation ground might refer to the place where bodies are burnt, or the Absolute, or a woman's genitals (yoni).

devoured by jackals or vultures. In his challenging article 'Intimate Relationship as a Spiritual Crucible', psychotherapist John Welwood elaborates on this image of a 'charnel ground' as a metaphor for a sacred relationship, in which both the hell and ecstasy of a deep relationship must be integrated in order to reach true communion. Embracing life involves acceptance of the realities of death, destruction and suffering.

Written texts came after sacred ritual practice, and the language is ambiguous, due to the secret nature of such practices.

Texts referring to the sacred union of Shiva and Shakti could be describing sexual intercourse, the union of male and female breaths within the body, or even occasionally an eclipse!

Principles of Tantra philosophy

Tantric esoteric teachings within Hinduism and Buddhism encompass a range of different practices, texts and interpretations. However, according to scholar Georg Feuerstein, they all have fundamental approaches in common and an emphasis on the need for an experienced teacher (or guru) who can initiate and guide followers.

Using fast track, unorthodox methods, spiritual realization is possible within a single lifetime, rather than many lifetimes. The use of sexual energy is one of these unorthodox methods, and it can be harnessed to drive spiritual transformation. The belief that kundalini energy lies dormant in every individual and can be awakened through yoga practices is fundamental to Tantric practices, which regard our individual body as a microcosm that replicates the important features of the macrocosm (the universe).

In conclusion, they hold that mind and matter – and everything that exists – are all manifestations of cosmic energy and so have a spiritual rather than material basis for reality.

The dark goddess Kali (a goddess thought rooted in the pre-Aryan days of the Indus civilization) represents the principles of Tantra at work in the material world which can be used as the grist for transformation.

Tara, a Boddhisatva, a being on the path to enlightenment making the gesture of protection.

The sexism of sexual rites

Among the Kula, the ritual known as kula-dravya is said to involve generating the sacred nectar created by the mingling of male semen, female sexual emissions and menstrual fluid. There is reputedly a Tantric tradition in which dozens of initiated couples re-create a cosmic wheel, in which they synchronously engage in ritual sex as a sacred rite.

Within certain esoteric strands of Buddhism, ritual sex may be prescribed in detail – although sex itself is in some ways considered incidental to the transcendent aims of sexual congress. In some traditions within Tantra, women's spiritual development may be subordinate to the aim of helping men use their sexual energy to transform themselves.

This Tibetan thangka depicts Kalachakra with his consort, and represents both the Tantric deity and the philosophies contained within the Kalachakra Tantra.

One text (the *Ganachakra*) even suggests the use of young girls, while women are described as energy providers. I suspect that these kinds of statements are related to the past use of prostitutes as partners for sexual practices, rather than female adepts, since Buddhism in particular has been dominated by the institutionalization of large numbers of monks. Patriarchal power structures are not necessarily challenged when women's role in mainstream society is of low status!

The darker side of ritual sex

The focus in sexual practice appears to be more about self-development than connecting with the partner. For this reason, some Tantric texts suggest unfamiliar women are preferred as partners for ritual sex.

A more recent report in *Time* magazine described the shocking story of an Indian villager who had told his wife to dress in her wedding clothes, adorned her forehead with silver lingam, and took her to a meeting of his Shakti sect, where 84 couples were due to take part in the kanchalia dharam, or 'ceremony of the blouse'. When the wife realized that she would have to have sex with whoever chose her blouse, she ran off, chased by her husband, who then cut off her nose for disobeying him. The story ended with her suicide.

This dark side of the practice of ritual sex should not be forgotten in our search for divinely inspiring sex. Tantra has been repackaged in the West as Neo-Tantra, in which the couple relationship is seen as a crucible for personal transformation and spiritual growth. However, older texts do describe practising couples as equals, although it is notable that female voices are missing from the textual record. One such female that survived was the woman in the poems by Saraha.

The story of Saraha

Saraha was an 8th century Bengali Buddhist monk castigated by the royal court as fallen, because he gave up celibacy and married a low-caste arrow-maker with whom he practised Tantric rites. In his own defence to the court, he recited a poem cycle that won him respect – both he and his wife were said to achieve enlightenment:

There is neither passion nor absence of passion.
Seated beside her own, her mind destroyed,
Thus I have seen the yogini.
That blissful delight that consists between lotus [vagina]
and vajra [thunderbolt/ penis],
Who does not rejoice there? This moment may be the bliss
of means, or of both wisdom and means.
It is profound, it is vast.
It is neither self nor other ...
Even as the moon makes light in black darkness,
So in one moment the supreme bliss removes all defilement.
When the sun of suffering has set,
Then arises this bliss, this lord of the stars.
It creates. with continuous creativity,
And of this comes the mandala [circle] of the cosmos.
Gain purification in bliss supreme,
For here lies final perfection.
From the Royal Songs of Saraha

Woman is the creator of the universe,
the universe is her form;
woman is the foundation of the world,
she is the true form of the body.
Whatever form she takes,
whether the form of a man or a woman,
is the superior form.
In woman is the form of all things,
of all that lives and moves in the world.
There is no jewel rarer than woman,
no condition superior to that of a woman.
There is not, nor has been, nor will be
any destiny to equal that of a woman;
there is no kingdom, no wealth,
to be compared with a woman;
there is not, nor has been, nor will be
any holy place like unto a woman.
There is no prayer to equal a woman.
There is not, nor has been, nor will be
any yoga to compare with a woman,
no mystical formula nor asceticism
to match a woman.
There are not, nor have been, nor will be
any riches more valuable than woman.

From the *Saktisangama Tantra*

The fire offering

Fire is a common symbol for the metaphor of transformation. Contemporary ayurvedic medical practitioners in India use medicinal substances such as ash derived from burning away of gross matter to reduce a substance to its essence. This alchemical procedure also inspires fire offerings, in which there are multiple layers of purification and transformation.

Fire offerings are common within Vedic Hinduism, but within Tantra they have a specific purpose – to burn away psychic impurities in order to facilitate spiritual development. Some forms of meditation imagine a fire in the centre of the navel, devouring negative attitudes and emotions, or past experiences – whatever is holding the person back. Symbols such as letters of the Sanskrit alphabet, or elements representing different layers of experience, may be visualized as consumed by the fire.

An advanced Tantric variation is to practise fire meditation during sexual union, cleansing impurities or habitual attachment to worldly concerns. In the Buddhist context, the fire meditation is used to consign all experiences to the realization of the fundamental emptiness behind the phenomenal world.

According to contemporary Canadian Buddhist nun Medhanandi, 'We stand in silent witness to emptiness – in the flame of no flame, in the cooling of the last ember.'

In the more earthy spirit of the Hindu Tantric tradition, one way of conceptualizing the fire offering is that men must sacrifice their sexual energy to the fire of sexual arousal in order for the couple to transform

An aghori ascetic, many of whom follow the tantra, or the path of direct experience of divinity. He uses a skull cap as a begging bowl, lives by the cremation grounds and meditates.

this base energy into more refined energy. A man's seed might be the offering for which, in return, he receives amrita, or golden nectar, a substance that appears to refer to sexual juices as the nectar that rains down on the world from the love-making of Shakti and Shiva.

The Vijnana Bhairava – Meditation Techniques

This text, a chapter from the ancient Rudrayamala Tantra, was translated by Paul Reps in his book *Zen Flesh, Zen Bones*, and contains some of the most beautiful and simple instructions for meditation practices. Appended to each quote is a commentary from contemporary Indian guru Osho on the relevance of the sexual symbolism of the fire mediation for contemporary relationships.

'At the start of sexual union, keep attention on the fire at the beginning, and so continuing, avoid the embers at the end.' (In Tantric union the goal is not orgasm – in fact, orgasm is to be avoided – in order to keep the attention on the fire created through your sexual energy and becoming identified with this energy rather than on sexual satisfaction. The idea that you remain with the beginning and forget about the end implies that sex is not just about release of tension, but about relaxing into the sexual flow and merging with the other. This provides a taste of non-duality – of oneness.)

'When in such embrace your senses are shaken as leaves, enter this shaking.' (Totally identify with the joint sexual experience ... and allow it to flow through you without controlling your feelings.)

'Even remembering union, without the embrace, the transformation,' (Once you have tasted bliss with your partner, you can recall it and enter it even when you are alone. Sexual energy can be used in this way to transform your experience of reality – into a vibrant field of energy in which you exist and fully participate.)

Life is pure energy

In yoga, the human body is viewed as a microcosm of the universe: all that exists in the universe exists also in the human body. The path to enlightenment lies in recognizing our connection to the dynamic unity of reality. Tantra is a means of developing greater awareness of reality, of entering life with passion and intensity. Tantra has become extremely popular in the West, partly because of the relevance of its message of self-understanding and development, but also because of

Making a sign for completion reminds us that we are in energy flow all the time – our thoughts and moods can be seen as just energy – whether they are positive or negative.

its reputation for deepening sexual experience and orgasmic capacity.

Neo-Tantra (see page 233) presents sex as a path to developing awareness of the kundalini energy of Shakti. However, practitioner Daniel Odier suggests that you have to develop a sense of passionate engagement with life and its dynamic energy before you can experience sex as a field of resonance in which you are connected not only with your sexual partner but with the life force itself. Otherwise, Tantric practices become an exotic means of achieving better orgasms rather than a doorway into a more intense experience of reality.

Tantra and the yoga of presence

Mainstream religion on the Indian subcontinent distinguishes between daily life and spiritual life, encouraging seekers to delay dedicating themselves to religious enquiry until they have passed the stage of householder in the life cycle, then to retire from the world and become an ascetic. In contrast, Tantra celebrates our lived experience in our body as reality itself.

Tantric initiate Daniel Odier describes the yoga of presence as the most crucial style of meditation to foster the ability to connect. Tantra exploration is not about transcending reality in order to go inside oneself, but about entering reality more fully. Experience is more intense if our senses are sharpened, which connects us more to the natural world, our bodies and others.

Senses are a gateway to rediscovering the world around us as vibrant and dynamic. In the Tantric description of life, it is a shimmering, dancing play of energy that we can experience if we enter that state of vitality and dynamic playfulness. This is another definition of bliss; which for many ascetics is a description of the fruits of spiritual enlightenment.

Bliss is about being fully immersed in your experience – both the world of the senses, the movement of energies, and a quality of attentive awareness to all this at once.

Being fully alive to the natural world, and the flow of energies with us and between us creates a powerful sense of presence.

Exercise: The practice of presence

Awareness through senses

Presence means to be present to one's own sensations, as well as to one's own thoughts and feelings. This practice is well established by Jon Kabat-Zinn as mindfulness (see page 212). The first step is to become more aware of your own body, which enables you to inhabit your body more fully and increase your awareness. Many practices start with breathing. You can develop this practice to become aware of the world through your senses, paying attention to the particular sensations around you: smell, taste, hearing, touch, sight and sound; listening to the sound of silence.

1 Start by paying attention to your breath as you breathe in, allowing it to fill your lungs and abdomen before you slowly exhale. Feel your breath in your belly; do not force anything: do not pull the breath in or push it out.

2 Simply move your attention to your breathing without suppressing your awareness of other things, whenever your mind starts to wander.

3 Sense your body – be aware of how it feels. Let everything else in your environment go to the edges of your awareness.

4 At any moment, you can choose to simply move your attention to your body. Focusing your awareness on your senses – how your body feels, and what is going on within it – enables you to inhabit your body more fully and increase your awareness of living in a body.

5 Become aware of what you're smelling, seeing, hearing, touching, sensing, thinking ...

Sex and separation

There are a number of possible reasons why sex and the spirit became separated. Social, economical and political realities have increasingly restricted the roles and lives of women, so that in contemporary society they are sometimes treated as chattels – or at least, second-class citizens. Where women have lost status and are neither initiated into a Tantric group nor treated as equals in any way, their participation in such rites becomes a travesty of the principles on which goddess worship is based. Another reason is connected with a long tradition of ascetic mendicants, who were usually solitary and celibate. In Buddhism, the semen is equated with the compassionate mind (bodhicitta) and aspirants are advised not to discharge it.

The spiritual realm is deemed superior, while the mortal realm is inherently flawed and in some ways irrelevant to the broader goal of transcending daily reality. Just as St Augustine's concept of life as being irredeemably full of suffering

has come to dominate the Judeo-Christian world view, so Buddhism casts daily life as suffering and prescribes practices to foster a sense of detachment from the daily round. The fact that there is an overall consensus in world religions does not mean that underlying assumptions are correct. If the spiritual view of non-duality – as propounded by enlightened teachers such as the Buddha – is correct, such distinctions collapse. Sacred sexuality can serve to counter a world view that makes our human lives seem insignificant and our sexual pleasures superficial.

Exercise: Practice of presence with another

The power of connection

You can practise this with a child, a friend, a lover. Connection with another person is about being totally aware of what is going on with them. It is not just about being there with the other person, but about tuning in to them and letting them simply be themselves.

1 Focus your attention on the other person, without analysing or judging them.

2 Encourage them to relax in your presence and notice that you are fully aware of them.

This may sound a bit vague, but the quality of paying full attention can be almost tangible to sensitive individuals. Many people can tell immediately if their partner's awareness starts wandering, as the sense of connection immediately weakens. It is important to be aware of the sensations and movements of energy inside ourselves, as well as our moods and emotions. Taking responsibility for our own feelings rather than blaming what we feel on someone else – or conversely, making them responsible for keeping us happy – means being aware of our sensory and energetic perceptions of others and having an openness to being influenced by or to receiving their energy. You can use meditations that incorporate body awareness to relax and identify with your body rather than with your mind.

Daoism and Tantra

Daoism (also written as Taoism), Buddhism and Confucianism are the three great religions/philosophies of Ancient China. Daoism started as a combination of psychology and philosophy, but evolved into a religious faith in 440 CE, when it was adopted as a state religion in China – remaining so until 1911. The Dao De Ching (*The Way of Virtue*), an influential and lyrical ancient Chinese classic text, was written by Lao Tse (604–531 BCE).

Dao can be defined as 'path'. The way of the Dao is the way of Nature. Nature and reality are one and the same. The Dao is often described as a force that flows through all life. A happy life is one that is in harmony with the Dao, with Nature. Man depends on Nature, and needs to understand the connection between life and reality to cultivate wisdom. We can think of the Dao as a ceaseless flow of energy that pools, eddies and moves in every direction, constantly changing. Energy is always in the process of changing into something else, and is unpredictable. The challenge for people is to go with the flow rather than try to keep things as they are.

Yin and yang

The ideal Daoist has learned to use all his senses to intuit the shapes of the currents of energy and go with the flow. He acts in complete harmony with them. Daoists see energy as yin and yang, female and male, but these energies are not fixed and separate, but fluid and complementary, always morphing into one another.

Yin and yang – the idea of opposites emerging out of complementaries and then feeding back in a compelling symbol of interdependence. The ending is already present in the beginning.

How Daoists circulate sexual energy

Daoist meditators circulate energy through the subtle body (which seems to be a simplified form of the Indian chakra system) to unite inner and outer in the great whole, the Dao. Transformation takes place in three energy centres: the belly, the solar plexus and behind the eyes. Energy has to pass through the lowest gate to the middle gate and finally the jade gate to enter the forehead. The breath is the instrument for arousing energy and then opening the gates.

The lowest energy centre, the tan t'ien, is visualized as containing a cauldron situated at the belly, which has to be heated with inner fire.

Using breath and pumping the pelvic muscles, this sexual energy (ching) is alchemically processed into vital energy (chi) in the middle centre and rises up to the forehead, where it is transformed into shen, which provides a cosmic sense of vision.

Using a deep in-and-out breathing, the meditator sends his breath in a cycle from the genitals up along the spine to the head and then down again towards the genitals, recycling the energy through his own body. As men are considered largely yang, the base energy can be stimulated though masturbation and sent upwards by squeezing the genitals. To rebalance his system, he requires some of the yin essence of a woman.

Daoist sexual alchemy

Daoist sexual alchemy involves drawing in female yin energy during sexual contact while sending yang energy into the woman, so that each partner receives an input of their opposite and complementary energy, which rebalances their whole system. The ching mixes and blends with the chi through the practice of breath and inner fire, until it joins with the shen at the level of the eyes. By rolling the eyes upwards the jade gate opens, releasing the energy into the crown, from where it flows down into the cauldron in the belly and is purified again.

When in the top energy centre (the shen), the energy is visualized as flowing into gold and silver, sol and luna, to produce the seed of immortality. The breath is held and the breathing forms the seed of a child, who will eventually emerge as an immortal at the crown of the skull. These ideas are similar to alchemical ideas already discussed about the creation of the philosopher's daughter through the union of opposites.

When Daoists experience the image of the immortal child at the crown of the skull, it is seen as an inner ascent through which they personally return to the original source of life.

Holding back from ejaculation

Daoism theorizes that regular loss of seed drains the body of basic energy and vitality and actually shortens your life. Daoists and Tantric practitioners have been advocating retention of the semen for centuries, and have developed techniques for recycling the ejaculatory impulse through the nervous system and using it to nourish the subtle body. Holding back from ejaculation encourages the development of a more sensitive sexual style, in which men can focus on the movement of sexual energy within their body and between them and their partner rather than on physical sensations. More important is the receptivity of each partner to the complementary energy of their partner. Daoist theory proposes that, during sexual connection, these energies can be passed to the other, where they are available for integration into the partner's energy body.

The dual cultivation of sexual energy for couples has been described in detail by Mantak Chia, a contemporary Daoist writer and teacher. Men learn to retain their semen while maintaining an erection for lengthy periods of time. Once the man has learned to retain his semen while maintaining an erection, the couple can redirect sexual energy throughout the energy channels described by the Daoist practitioners, rather than focusing on genital stimulation and orgasmic satisfaction.

Technique of the big draw

In the big draw the aim is to prevent chi, or life force, escaping from the body during sexual arousal and especially in semen.

First, men strengthen the muscles of the pelvic floor by raising their testicles. During sexual arousal, the excitement is drawn from the penis by squeezing the pelvic floor, focusing on the area of the anus while holding the breath. Energy created in the genitals is then imagined as being pumped or drawn up the spine to the belly and on to the head, where it circulates. The spiralling seminal energy is then imagined as flowing down into the mouth as golden nectar. As men release and relax, they release a wave of yang (heavenly) sexual energy to flow down through the body and into the woman.

A woman's sexual energy is conceived of as yin (earthly) and during sexual intercourse she draws in yang energy, which complements her own energy. Men receive the woman's yin energy expelled though her vagina, which is a vital complement to their own.

According to Daoist philosophy, sex involves the exchange of yin and yang energies to create an integrated energy within each person's subtle body.

Shaivism and Shaktism in Tantra tradition

In the Tantric view of the world, there are two distinct planes within absolute reality. The transcendental plane is described as pure consciousness and is represented by Shiva, the male principle. The active (immanent) plane of matter is known as Shakti, the female principle. Without Shakti, the animating female principle of the universe, Shiva is regarded as static, a potentiality. Shaivism and Shaktism are two of the major sects of Hinduism, and Shiva and Shakti are usually worshipped as complementary equals within Shiva cults. The universe with all its forces of creation, preservation and dissolution is experienced as the play of Shakti.

Tantric yogis meditate on pure consciousness as Shiva (or Brahman), and on creation as Shakti (or Kali). Meditating on their union brings the two aspects of creation into dynamic relationship.

During the Tantric ritual of sexual union (maithuna), the woman represents the goddess Shakti and, as the active principle, she takes an active sexual role.

The phallus of Shiva is erect because it is raised to full consciousness, and in full consciousness it penetrates the universe.
The vulva of Shakti is open, because in full consciousness she lets the universe penetrate her ... At the core of their mutual penetration supreme consciousness reigns.
From *Tantric Quest* Daniel Odier

V.R.CHIDAMBARAM
SIVAGANGAI

*The ubiquitous yoni-lingam in the form of a natural upright stone is
the representation of Shiva in meditative posture.*

Shaivism

Evidence of Shiva cults has been found in ancient archaeological sites of
Harappa and Mohenjo Daro, on the banks of the river Indus, in present-
day Pakistan. Around 700–1000 CE, Shaivism become prominent in the
south of India, partially due to the patronage of ruling chieftains who
dedicated beautiful temples to Shiva. The earliest recorded Shaivite
Upanishad dates from around 400 BCE. Shakti is depicted as the consort
of Shiva, and their sexual congress is venerated as a means of sustaining
the universe, while individual sexual rites are followed to raise and
concentrate the primal life force.

The wandering ascetics

In the cult of the god Shiva, he is identified with the human faculty of
consciousness. Shaivism centres on linga puja, a ceremony honouring
such qualities in the form of a phallus. Devotees wear a phallic-shaped
lingam, and make offerings to the lingam, which stands for Shiva's potent
energy. Shiva has an ascetic aspect, and many followers are celibate,
following austere meditation practices in the Himalayas, an area
associated with Shiva. Wandering ascetics may carry tridents or mark
their forehead with three lines to represent the third eye (inner wisdom)
of Shiva, and carry rosaries of beads to represent the tears of Rudra –
the destructive aspect of Shiva. Wandering teachers and followers live
on offerings, by the grace of God. Devotees also smear holy ash taken
from a cremation ground, on their bodies for protection and purification,
considering ash to symbolize the semen of fire, and some smoke cannabis
as an offering.

The forehead of this Shaivite ascetic is marked with the sign of wisdom.

Shaktism and goddess worship

Shakti treats matter and spirit as integrated, and especially celebrates matter. The world of body and flesh is not avoided as one of illusion (maya) and entanglement, but is a manifestation of the dance of the divine. In fact, the fundamental energy of the universe is sexual – and the whole universe is seen as the manifestation of Shakti energy. Shakti refers to the immanent goddess power, which chooses to manifest itself, the primal creative principle underlying the cosmos, which energizes every living thing; the masculine element is said to be transcendent. Shakti energy is usually described as a dynamic, vibrational energy state.

If Shiva stands for consciousness, Shakti is the dynamic principle that imbues consciousness with life.

Shaktism is probably the oldest form of Hinduism. According to archaeological evidence, the Goddess was worshipped in this region at least 20,000 years ago, in the upper Paleolithic period. In the Son valley of northern India, archaeologists found a rectangular platform with natural concentric circles installed in the centre dating from Paleolithic times. This Upper Palaeolithic monument is known locally as the Shrine of Kalika Mai (Mother Kali).

Another monument in the same area is the prehistoric Kerai Ki Devi shrine. Such monuments date from as early as 8000 to 200 BCE and suggest a remarkably long continuity of mother goddess worship. Thousands of terracotta figurines from the Neolithic period (5500 BCE) have been found at Mehrgarh, in modern-day Baluchistan (south-west Pakistan), which pre-dates the Indus Valley civilization of Harappa. None of the texts from the early period of Shakti cult has survived to

This 16th-century bronze statue of the goddess Parvati, the consort of Shiva. She is another manifestation of Shakti.

the present day, although a number of texts date from post-Buddhist times to about 1200 CE. Shaktism was not a literate text-based tradition, like most popular forms of religion in the Far East.

While Shakti features in the *Vedas*, it is in the Tantras that she appears to take the role of the supreme force of creation. Customs and rituals have been handed down in the oral tradition for millennia – and worship has an extremely broad and popular base. The entrances to domes and dolmens are thought to resemble the great mother's 'passage' (the Sanskrit word for sanctuary means womb chamber), while vessels were often used in ritual practice to symbolize the making of life, birth and rebirth. The genital areas of sculptures were – and still are – regarded as the source of all life and focus of the goddess's energy and touched with reverence.

Exercise: Meditation - meeting the mother

The divine mother

Tantra has roots in archaic forms of goddess worship, and incorporates natural features such as fire, 'menstruating' rivers, the womb as a sacred space and sexual fluids. A suitable place to encounter the Divine Mother may be in an underground cave. Using active imagination, use this guided meditation to come face to face with the goddess, and experience her love.

1 After a few minutes sitting relaxed, close your eyes and imagine that you are standing in front of an awesome cave.

2 Enter the cave, and follow the passage that leads downward, into the womb of the earth. Notice how it feels warm and nurturing ...

3 Go deeper still, until you find yourself in the very core, the heart of the earth ...

4 Become aware that you are expected, that a powerful force is here in the centre of the earth as you enter into the presence of the mother goddess.

5 Spend some time looking at her and acknowledging her magnificence. Feel the loving energy radiating from her heart and absorb it.

6 Feel your own heart open and expand as your consciousness blends with hers. Feel the sacred energy filling every part of you, energizing you. You now are one with this radiant being.

7 Slowly as you're ready, carry the radiant love of the Divine Mother in your own heart.

8 Begin the return journey from the core of the earth, through the cave and into the daylight. Take some time to reflect on your experience.

The feminine energy

The goddess is known by various names in different parts of India, and takes many forms in Hinduism – Shakti, Devi, Durga, Parvati, Kali and other locally worshipped goddesses. Devi comes from the Sanskrit root div, meaning 'to shine'.

These myriad goddesses are all regarded as different manifestations of the great goddess. She represents the creative force in the world, the force that galvanizes the divine ground of existence into self-projection as the cosmos. Within the Tantric esoteric tradition the feminine energy, or Shakti, is considered to be the immanent force behind all action and existence in the phenomenal cosmos.

Followers of Shakti often practise devotional or bhakti yoga. For those on the bhakti path, love is a form of worship. The feminine principle pervades creation, and is often personified as a loving mother. She is to be adored with intensity, while the devotee dissolves the self by focusing intently on the true reality underlying time, space and causation.

Healing your own relationship with your mother, and seeing her as representative of the archetype of mothering, can open the door to acknowledging the divinity of mothering. Buddhist teacher Deshung Rinpoche believes that regardless of how your later relationship may have fared, mothers should be honoured for having given us the gift of life, and their devotion to us as babies.

This painted scroll, or thangka, depicts the Green Tara, Buddhist goddess of universal compassion and enlightened action.

Worshipping the yoni

Yoni is a Sanskrit word for the vagina, which in ancient Tantra symbolized the sacred temple of the goddess. Invoking Shakti through yoni worship (puja) is an established path towards the goal of merging with the divine.

Yoni Tantra (a 16th-century Bengali text) is a sacred scripture for initiates of the Tantra tradition, since it is the celebration of the Tantra goddess.

According to contemporary neo-Tantra teacher Subhojit Dasgupta, the ordinary rules for Tantra worship are suspended for the one who follows magical Shakti precepts. This verse from the Shakti Tantra demonstrates the true meaning behind yoni worship:

> *'There is not, nor has been,*
> *nor will be*
> *any holy place like unto*
> *a woman.'*

It is thought by some that the earliest strand of Tantra yoga focuses on yoni puja, a ceremony honouring the vulva – either of a

Yoni lingam puja reminds the worshipper of the individual two-in-oneness of male and female from which all life originates.

statue or a living woman – that involves making offerings of food and liquids while chanting prayers, or sexually arousing a woman while she embodies the goddess Shakti. Shaivism centres on linga puja, a ceremony honouring the penis, often in the form of a natural upright stone.

The creation, maintenance, and destruction of the universe – all originate in the Yoni.

Absorb yourself in the yoni through meditation,
with yoni on the tongue,
yoni in the mind,
yoni in the ears,
and yoni in the eyes.
All spiritual practice is useless without the yoni.
Therefore ... worship the Yoni.
From the *Yoni Tantra*

In these secret rituals, the vulva of a woman is worshipped as a symbol of the goddess. Some sculptures depict worshippers drinking sublime essence from the yoni, considered one of the most sacred substances. Sexual fluids can be tasted as a means of absorbing the charged energy of those substances. In the middle chamber of the Kamakhaya Shakti temple in Assam, a cave forms the inner sanctum, from which an underground spring flows through a yoni-shaped cleft in the rock. It seems incredible to us (or shocking, with our taboos on menstrual blood) that during summer, when the water runs red with iron oxide, it is ritually drunk as symbolic of the menstrual blood of the goddess. The 'menstruating' rock is worshipped as Shakti's genitals.

In this Shakti cult, the taboo against menstruating women is broken down – the menstrual fluid is regarded as sacred. Menstruating women are venerated during ritual practice for the charged state of their bodily energy, in which they are manifesting the essence of femininity – represented by the redness of the discharge. Red is the colour associated with the goddess, while white is the colour of masculine awareness (and semen). Many rituals are based on uniting the red and the white. Menstruating women were considered particularly potent energetically, and were regarded as sexual initiators. During menstruation women are identified with the goddess Kali, who rules over life, death and rebirth. As such, Kali is in contact with other worlds, beyond space and time, and sexual union with her can help the adept access this realm. During intercourse, the menstruating woman rides her partner, like the prostate - even dead - Shiva she rides sexually. In this ritual, lips refer to yoni:

When he has embraced his partner and inserted his sceptre
into her lotus, he should drink heavily from her lips,
which are brushed with milk.
As the full richness of delight is enjoyed her thighs begin to quiver
and her first fulfilment is reached.
This is the way of becoming one with the imperishable – by absorbing
each other selflessly.

From the *Kalachakra Tantra*

Tantra and red

Stencilled image of a Bodhisattva at the monastery of Wat Sensoukharam, Laos.

According to Tantric practitioner Daniel Odier:

> *There is only one colour in Tantra. Red is the colour of the living heart, the colour of blood, the colour of fire, the colour of roses and the tongues, the colour of the open vulva, and the colour of the erect penis, the colour of the sun that warms the hermit, and the colour of the circle of the fire that must be crossed to attain consciousness.*

In the Shakti rituals of Tantric worshippers, the sacred essence contained in menstrual fluid may also be taken as a ritual drink along with (red) wine. There is even a vessel shaped like a yoni, which is used for libations – the ritual pouring of fluids over an altar during worship. In these left-hand rituals, the female is seated on the left – but she is considered the stronger force, as she embodies the sacred feminine and energizes the male on her right. The eternal dynamic energy of God is considered feminine while the male principle of form (Shiva) is considered static without the animating energy of Shakti to invigorate it.

With his head resting between her thighs, the adept drinks deeply
from the source of life. Above, the goddess causes his power to grow
and transform into the wisdom fields inside her mind, while below,
he enters each wave of wisdom according to his ability. Each
meditates on the transcendental experience of non-duality, until the
confluence of rivers swells and bursts its banks.

From the *Chandamaharosana Tantra*

In a ritual described in the Koka Shastra, the vulva (yoni) is smeared with honey prior to cunnilingus. There is much in Tantric texts about sexual juices as the elixir of life, although whether these are female ejaculate or the vaginal secretions of arousal is unclear. Sometimes the union of male and female juices, the amrita, or nectar, in which the white and the red elements are mixed is meant to be sipped; other rituals involve the menstrual blood, which is thought to contain powerful feminine essence.

During sex an alchemical process occurs in which the red primal material of sexuality is processed by the rest of the energy body, and transformed into its spiritual essence. This happens by mixing the red and the white elements that make up the metabolism of female and male bodies. This divine alchemy only takes place when couples unite in

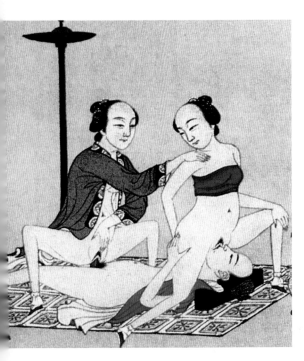

A graphic illustration of the Taoist 'joining of essences', entitled 'Celebration of Love' c. 1900. Women's sexual satisfaction was deemed to be essential and had the important result of intensifying sexual energy.

communion. These rituals are esoteric, so we only have access to snippets of information about what actually goes on, and can only hazard guesses at the meanings of such rituals for those involved. The descriptions we have access to are beautiful and they appear to be reverential.

On the other hand, adepts such as Daniel Odier have hinted at the sometimes extreme and shocking nature of such rituals and their power to permanently change your relationship to both sex and reality. They are naturally not widespread today.

Meditation on the yoni

In another Tantric ritual, the woman's genitals are depicted as a mandala, radiating out from the cervix to include her vulva and, from there, the whole woman. A mandala is a map of cosmic energies, and Tantric mandalas represent the different energies manipulated during ritual practice or meditation.

During a Buddhist variation of the ritual, the woman might focus on her own innate purity, wisdom and bliss, and imagine these qualities as emanating from her genitals. She gradually expands her awareness until it encompasses the whole of creation.

A couple's variation of the ritual

A man can help the woman focus in her meditation by tracing the eight nerves believed to radiate from the vagina with his forefinger, in order to wake them up (arouse them). These eight nerves are named after eight goddesses, and in arousing them, he invokes these goddesses.

The woman concentrates on drawing the awakened energy into her central channel, which directs the energy upwards, through her navel, heart and head, following the way energy flow is mapped onto the genitals. The man connects the tip of his penis with her cervix to create a circuit for the mingling of her red essence with his white essence. The couple concentrate on combining their energy to produce subtle states of bliss and awareness. According to the Guhyasamaja Tantra, an early Buddhist text, the man visualizes mandalas streaming out of his body as his sexual juices flow. The woman inhales the wind in her central energy channel, drawing it to the top of her head, imagining drops of nectar released into her being. She revels in their sexual pleasure and expands her consciousness – 'enjoying the sky'. For Buddhists, all benefits gained through any practices are dedicated to the development of the world and sentient beings.

> *Having created her, [the god Prajapati] worshipped her sexual organ; Therefore, a woman's vulva should be worshipped. He stretched forth from himself a stone for pressing nectar. And impregnated her with that....*

Stone relief graphically representing a woman's vulva, 10th century, India.

Venerating vajra

Vajra means both diamond and thunderbolt, both of which represent enlightened consciousness. The way of the Buddhist Tantric path known as Vajrayana is to spurn illusion and to take refuge in Buddhism – not through fear and self-effacement, or desire and arrogance, or through flight from the daily rounds of pleasure and pain, but by uncovering the diamond-like clarity of conscious awareness. Buddhists meditate on an enlightened being such as the Buddha in order to foster vajra-like qualities. Vajra also stands for the phallus – rather like the sword of the medieval Christian tradition, which stood for masculinity, while the chalice stood for the feminine wisdom of love. Vajra is used in a similar way to lingam, in Shaivite Tantra.

In ritual sex practices, many Tantras recommend that men hold back the semen together with the breath and the mind. All these qualities are seen as energies that can be cycled within the body to enable realized states of awareness. According to Buddhist Tantras, semen also embodies the 'enlightenment mind' and so it should not be discharged.

The yoga of fulfilment

Part of the Dzogchen esoteric tradition in Tibetan Buddhism, the yoga of fulfilment is concerned with sublime perfection, and involves advanced meditation practices. The 'perfection stage' is the last one in the yoga of fulfilment, before adepts realize their goal – a state of pure awareness that is both conscious and blissful. Buddhists call this the rainbow body.

Meditating on the subtle anatomy of veins and channels, the meditator develops an awareness of the energy body and creates drops of nectar. Through the process of meditation, the energy body is cleansed. The kinds of things that are cleared throughout this process could be emotional states, ignorance and misconceptions, or karmic bonds to the past.

According to Tantric philosophy, physical bodies are not solid. They are composed of different elements, which combine to form the winds and drops of fluid that move through the energy body. These elements can be shared with a love partner, exchanged and recombined to constitute an expanded body. When integrated with that of your partner, the combined energy body is even more potent. Male and female genitals are charged with different energies, like an electrical charge, and connecting them increases this charge.

The Dorje or Vajra is the Tibetan equivalent of the lingam.

Exercise: Tantra meditation – deity yoga

Identifying with the Buddha

A core meditative practice of Vajrayana Buddhism is to visualize oneself as Buddha, the purpose being to realize that you and the deity are essentially the same. The meditation usually starts with a reminder of the void, as you imagine the familiar world completely dissolving. Then you can expand into the space of emptiness; your mind can unwind and rest in dynamic relaxation. Try it yourself. You can use a painting of your favourite deity, or a Buddha if you prefer to identify with an enlightened being.

1 After entering a state of meditation (as described above), simply sit and gaze at the image for some time. Observe everything about the deity, and imagine their qualities as part of yourself. Allow their qualities to take over more and more, until the deity inhabits you, dissolving your own personality and ego.

2 Realize that the form of the deity is merely a form for an energetic principle – or consciousness, if you prefer – and let your sense of yourself as a person sitting and meditating dissolve into the exercise itself. If the meditation is part of the quality of universal consciousness, allow that consciousness to enter you so that your consciousness becomes part of a pervasive universal consciousness.

3 Gradually allow the identification with universal consciousness to arise spontaneously, without having to make it happen. Rest in the emptiness behind all forms whenever you can.

Kali, sex and death

In south India, the Shakti traditions constellate around the hugely popular cult of the goddess Kali (which means time). Kali is a terrible and vibrant manifestation of the archetypal dark goddess, who is also worshipped with devotion as a loving mother (Kali-ma). Possibly because of the mother goddess's intimate relationship with the mysteries of birth, death – and death in childbirth – she is seen to have power over life and death.

Kali was a shape-shifter, who is most well known in her terrifying guise of a machete-wielding force, wearing a garland of human heads and drinking from a human skull. She represents both the creative and destructive aspects of nature, because she is deemed responsible for all of life, from conception to death, and has power over all. The cyclical nature of life and death is represented by her garland of human heads and the unpredictable visitation of disaster by the blood dripping from their severed necks, which also drips from the machete she wields. Kali's dishevelled hair represents the chaos from which life emerged.

Kali is a figure of pure potent energy. Clothed with the veil of space, her blue-black nakedness symbolizes the night of non-existence (a night that is free of illusion). As dark night, Kali is the destroyer of time, and she also represents the fire in which worlds can be dissolved, just as bodies are burnt at the cremation ground.

Associated particularly with the Kula school of Tantrics, Kali is also depicted as lover, beloved and devourer of the god Shiva. She contains all opposites – in extreme form – within her. Death and love, in the Tantric tradition, are two sides of the same coin.

Kali the dark goddess

In the *Kulachudamani Tantra*, the magical side of Kula and Kali worship is dwelt on in great detail, wit`h references to sacrifice and siddhis (magical powers) – including a mysterious process where the Tantric adept leaves his body at night so that he can engage in sexual intercourse with Shakti.

According to Indian author Ajit Mukherjee, the terrifying representation of the dark Goddess is a symbol that embodies the unity of the transcendental. Kali is another aspect of Shakti, and as her name indicates, she stands for timelessness and the space within which all forms and illusions are destroyed. Kali demonstrates the age-old power of the goddess in her dark aspects. Older goddesses could be demanding and wrathful, and are not always identified with love, joy and bliss. They ruled over death and the struggle for life. As both creator and destroyer, her world is an eternal flux in which all things arise and then disintegrate.

Kali dancing on Shiva, 19th century. Her hands represent the principle of karma; one hand wields a sword to cut through illusion, while the other carries the severed head of the ego identity.

The birth of neo-Tantra

Many modern Tantra teachers in the West trained with Rajneesh (1931–90), or under students of his, and it is his message that has been hugely influential in the burgeoning field of neo-Tantra, the Westernized interpretations of Tantra focusing on sex and self-development.

As well as his exploration of Eastern teachings, Rajneesh incorporated many elements broadly drawn from 1960s-style psychotherapy practices, such as encounter groups, the primal scream and body work (such as that of Wilhelm Reich), in a style that emphasized catharsis, liberation from social conditioning, and freedom of self-expression. Like other self-styled cult leaders who have fallen into the trap of power, Rajneesh and his inner circle were the subject of allegations of greed, nepotism and

paranoia. Rajneesh was a hugely charismatic teacher who synthesized traditional Indian beliefs into a form hugely attractive and accessible to Westerners. Now renamed Osho, his message of infusing sex with the song of the spirit, in particular, continues to prove irresistible.

Group practice at the Osho commune, in Pune, Western India.

Popular style

For several decades now, yoga and Tantric practices have influenced meditation, body work, energy sessions, sexuality, dance and yoga. Scholars see this kind of 'Californian Tantra' as a reimagining of ancient traditions, which have been stripped of their cultural associations and the hierarchies of knowledge that are part of the institutional practice of any religion – even one as amoral as some of the Tantric sects.

Neo-Tantra and other programmes that promise induction into sacred sex have adapted Eastern ideas and practices for the West, and linked them to a body-positive programme that affirms and celebrates sexuality as an expression of our fundamental nature. This chimes with a modern emphasis on the couple relationship as a crucible within which the dross of emotional discord can be alchemically transformed into the sublime. The Tantric sex movement has positioned itself as the means to do this, drawing from the message of Tantric gurus that such a path could provide a fast track to spiritual realization.

The field of neo-Tantra in America and Europe has recently become crowded with all sorts of teachers and self-styled healers – and in some instances healers wish to deliver healing through their hands, in the increasingly popular delivery of Tantric genital massage. Such practices are outside the established conventions of massage and therapy, and might be seen to stray into the field of sexual surrogacy.

Sex as a gateway

According to British teacher John Hawken, sex itself is a means for experiencing life as unified and blissful. Sex is both a metaphor and a gateway into an experience of the divine, because it is the area in our daily life in which we are most able to let go of the illusion of a separate self and merge into something that is larger than us.

The experience of ecstasy can happen naturally in the moment of orgasm or sexual union. The split between the experiencer and the experience is transcended, and there is a moment of oneness. In this way, pleasure can provide a direct path towards the consciousness of bliss.

For Hawken, 'There is no separation between life and spirituality. Tantra invites us consciously to explore these two energies that have the power to turn our lives upside down, to overthrow our best laid plans, and instead of trying to control or suppress them, to open to them, to surf them. In this way, we can use their energy to pursue our path of personal transformation and of liberation from ignorance and suffering, and to grow into our greatness and our spiritual dimension.'

Realizing oneness

In the same way that we need to take responsibility for our own emotions such as anger, we can take responsibility for whether we choose to experience bliss or not. This is a radical idea. If our nature is one of bliss, then the fact that we access it during sex is not an attribute of sex but something within us that arises spontaneously when we open up to the possibility of experiencing bliss through sex.

Erotic sculptures from the Khajuraho temple, India

The ultimate goal of Tantra, then, is realization of oneness, not sexual bliss in the genital way we know it. Bliss is not about orgasm but about oneness. By focusing on the meditative aspects of sexual experience, we can experience one another as a gateway to an expanded sense of consciousness in which we feel part of the oneness of life.

As the Eastern traditions we've looked at imply, realization involves an awareness of oneself where the experience of duality has collapsed into a sense of unity; this is not so much euphoric as a state of profound self-acceptance.

Making Sex Sacred

Practical Pathways to Bliss

What makes sex great?

Great sex makes you feel nurtured and leads to even more commitment to your relationship. If you want more sex, focus on quality, not quantity! Great sexual experiences feed your appetite for sensual enjoyment and deepen your attachment to your partner through the bonding emotions of love and closeness.

Eroticism involves far more than the meeting of two bodies, however passionate. The underlying meaning of the erotic principle is one of connection, whether it is between people, within individuals, or within communities.

The best sex is the sex during which you open yourself to love. When you integrate passion, heart, mind and soul, sex becomes great. In order to open up emotionally, you may need to let go of any anxiety you have about rejection or abandonment, as it is hard to achieve a state of flow when you're holding back for any reason. Letting go of your fear of exposing your vulnerability allows you to reveal yourself – and since your partner is often feeling just as vulnerable as you are, it may help you both to relax. If you've had commitment issues in the past, anxiety and fear just might even be a sign of a deeper intimacy emerging – and intimacy is a core ingredient of good sex.

Sexual energy flows through your body

Good sex involves letting the mind go and expressing your feelings through your body. It also involves letting energy flow through your being. It means attuning to your partner and allowing the connection between

The best sex is a heady mix of refined sensation, intimate flow and loving connection.

you to take its own shape – which may vary from day to day. The trick is to be free of expectations, as these tend to limit your possibilities.

Along with a sense of relaxation and playfulness comes increased energy, which you can use to enhance your relationship or to creatively feed into the experience of your day. If you are not in a relationship right now, you can still generate positive sexual energy and let that flow through you in order to nourish your daily life.

Eroticism encompasses pleasurable body sensations and positive emotions such as love, compassion and empathy, as well as spiritual energies such as connection and devotion. It's these kind of qualities that infuse sexual pleasure with meaning. The truth is that, as is the case with other areas in other areas of lives, what we get out of sex is dependent on what we put in.

How You Know it's Love!

Acceptance of both yourself and the other person is fundamental to love.

To create more love, pay attention to how your partner is feeling and remain open to the spontaneous play of energy between you.

Love is something that you create and constantly re-create, moment by moment.

Love is an energy, although you experience it as emotional attachment.

Love arises in you spontaneously – and it is within your power to generate more whenever you choose.

Love depends more on your own internal state than on how someone else feels about you.

Connection – attuning yourself to someone else – is at the heart of love.

Love requires empathy.

Love involves surrender.

Love can be defined as opening your heart to your beloved, without making demands or expecting something in exchange.

In love, you drop conditions and expectations.

Love requires you to be flexible, accepting that feelings rise and fall in intensity and can change over time.

Love evades attempts to control it; it requires you to stop grasping.

The importance of communication

To improve sex, you need to feel comfortable with your partner so that you can openly share your experience and talk with ease. Great sex evolves through a shared journey of self-discovery and unfolding sensuality within a trusting and safe relationship. Knowledge of the mechanics of sex and stages of sexual arousal, which have been available since the work of the early sex therapists such as Masters and Johnson, provide useful starting points on your sexual journey. From then on a range of other methods, drawn from the personal growth movement, can help to harmonize your love-making and inspire you.

Sex re-education

Sacred sex is highly attractive to people who intuitively know that there's more to sex than their early experiences may have offered, and who want to go beyond the limits of traditional sex. If you are in a loving relationship, you might choose to explore the sacred dimension intuitively, with the help of books or by consulting a sex therapist who knows about this area. You might even choose to sample workshops, if you're feeling confident and adventurous. But even if you're not in a relationship, you can still explore sacred sex by starting to work with your own sexual attitudes.

Our parents and our society, however, may not have trained us for the complex art of relating, nor for good love-making. In our culture, many young men condition themselves to respond sexually to images (and increasingly, to pornography) rather than to experience sexual feelings as a response to the deepening intimacy of an evolving friendship. Regular consumers describe how viewing porn empties their relationships of desire and arousal, leading them to require ever-greater levels of visual stimulation.

In the absence of real, open communication about sex and relationships, many individuals have learnt a sexual style in which they think mainly of their own physical gratification, with minimal regard for their partner's pleasure. Couples can get stuck at a relatively dysfunctional level of sexual interaction for many years. Honest and helpful feedback from sexual partners is often lacking. This limits

opportunities to explore sexuality honestly, which is a shame, as good sex can nourish connection and encourage even better communication. Many people have written of the dangers of reducing the meaning of Eros, to pure 'sex', contributing to its conversion to a mere commodity; a 'thing' to be bought and sold.

True, eros tends to rise 'in ecstasy' towards the Divine, to lead us beyond ourselves; yet for this very reason it calls for a path of ascent, renunciation, purification and healing. Benedict XVI, Deus Caritas Est

Love versus sex

Sex can be selfish. Too often, we expect our partners to gratify our sexual needs and get annoyed if they don't make love as much as we want to or don't initiate sex. If you take responsibility for your own sexual satisfaction, your mate is more likely to be receptive sexually when your desire to make love is motivated by a sense of loving connectedness.

Rewiring the brain

Different parts of the brain are involved in processing sex and love. Love appears to be much more powerful than sex in its effects on the brain, because it activates complex neural pathways and involves parts of the brain that are rich in dopamine, a chemical heavily associated with emotions and reward mechanisms.

Sex therapists and therapists of many persuasions believe that love is a skill that we often need to relearn. According to the findings of neuro-scientists, when we are in love or in any close supportive relationship, the possibility of rewiring our brains to process emotions and experience things in a different way is much stronger.

As we will see later (see page 348), studies of the brain function of experienced meditators show that we can profoundly change the way we experience things. Ecstasy may be just such an experience, one for which we can prepare ourselves. Social historian Roy Porter calls this process, in which we can create and define our own pleasures from our own unique viewpoint, 'the erotics of the imagination'. Tantra, and neo-Tantra in the West, reminds us you can learn these skills and reach ecstasy.

Ecstasy can be reached by yourself or with a partner, once you have learned the skills of love-making.

What is the experience of sacred sex?

Sacred sex involves a change of focus from going after your own pleasure (and power) to devoting yourself to your partner and an appreciation of their finer qualities. It involves seeing the universal, transcendent qualities of your relationship as part of a more fundamental way of understanding what it means to be deeply connected to one another. This often leads to a more caring relationship with everyone around you and a more active engagement in looking after others.

Some couples describe deep intimacy with their lover as naturally leading to euphoria. People describe such experiences of ecstasy in terms of a pervasive sense of mystical union, leading to deep and often lasting feelings of serenity and wholeness.

Tantric lovers start their ritual with a 'bow', acknowledging each other as divine.

Sacred Sex for Lovers

The heart of sacred sex for modern lovers is to use the model of sacred sex to imbue your relationship with loving connection. Tantric sex teaches you to tune in to your partner and use your sexual chemistry to feel at one with each other. It involves:

Bringing the sacred into your bedroom – create a sacred space

The art of creating ecstasy in your love life

Transcending egotism in your relationship by focusing on the transpersonal aspects of each other

Respecting and honouring your partner as you wish to be treated

Creating a deep heart connection

Starting foreplay before you even touch each other

Cultivating whole-body sensuality and awakening your senses

Using sexual energy as a form of meditation to achieve states of bliss.

As we have seen, in a variety of mystical traditions these ecstatic feelings can be allied to a broadly religious or spiritual world view.

Although ritual sex is often firmly embedded in a culturally specific and complex world view, in which sexuality is one way of mastering the sex drive and using it as a sort of motor for spiritual development, there is a lot of inspiration to be gained for couples who are not spiritual seekers.

Exercise:
Healing a blocked relationship

Re-energize through imagination

This exercise uses active imagination to re-create your relationship in the way you would love it to be. Doing this, you gain insight into the fact that changing the mood between you has tangible effects on your energy.

1 Choose a point of conflict with your partner and spend a few moments conjuring up how awful this is. For instance, if you're living in a no-sex relationship, imagine yourselves lying tense in the same bed too scared to mention the problem.

2 Imagine yourself as if you are your partner and try to see the lack of loving sex from their point of view – feel your way into their experience. After some time, extend your awareness to how your partner experiences you in this situation. This can be a revelatory experience, if you drop your own issues.

3 After some minutes shift your awareness back to your own body and breathing, fully relaxing. You are back in your own body and your own consciousness. Notice how different your body feels.

4 Imagine that the situation has been resolved. Luxuriate in the details of how this would impact on your daily life together. Imagine each interaction permeated with a lively sensuality and attraction. Let your awareness enter all the areas you are concerned with – including all your ways of communicating.

5 Close the meditation by coming back to your own body and breathing, and then spend some minutes reflecting on how to change the way you relate to your partner, right now.

The couple relationship

Sacred sex is currently seen as being primarily about relationship rather than about religiosity or spiritual growth. Choosing sacred sex means committing to growth and mutual exploration in a conscious, loving way, rather than simply creating a ritual setting for sex.

A relationship like this involves starting from a place where you feel good in yourself, rather than wanting the other person to complete you; where you feel independent, yet interdependent – because you're with your partner by choice. This means being able to accept and tolerate difference without threatening the relationship every time things aren't going your way. You both have an awareness of your own needs and take responsibility for meeting these needs, changing your own attitudes rather than expecting the other person to change theirs.

You see communication as a dance of energy, rather than as something fixed or inflexible. You see love as an energy that you sustain through what you do together and you recognize that the flow of energy between you is more important than being right. Having a magical, caring, loving, joyful relationship means making a commitment to doing whatever it takes to maintain a great connection – usually spending time together talking and working things out.

Tantric sex provides a model of a loving relationship in which you are more embodied – living in your senses, open-hearted and more sexually engaged. Your love-making embraces sensuality, whole-body pleasure, loving connection and a sense that sex can be a gateway to a bonded and on-going connectedness.

Your partner is your companion on the journey of development. Treat them as your friend – each of you will grow in your own way, and at your own pace.

By immersing yourself in a loving, whole-hearted relationship you can use sex to reinvigorate the relationship, to open your capacity for sexual pleasure and to bond more deeply. The ideas we looked at in the last chapter suggest that an awareness of sex as energy can revitalize your daily experience as more vibrant, pleasurable and even joyful.

Through love-making with a sense of the divine you become co-creators, remaking your joint world in the way you wish it to be.

The myth of romantic love

Living in a culture where the sacred is increasingly marginalized by mainstream religions and where the vast majority of people no longer identify with a religious world view, the romantic couple has become a central icon. It is now the couple relationship that, for many of us, carries our hopes and expectations for fulfilment on physical, emotional and spiritual levels. We imagine that romance can get us through relationship difficulties and that more romance is the answer to sexual distance. As our expectations increase, the ability to create intimacy and sustain meaningful relationships can be stretched to breaking point.

The concept of relationship needs to be broader; sometimes it's about partnership, sometimes it's a private and intense connection with your self-awareness, self-knowing, the ability to touch your own body or emotions. At other times it could refer to a relationship with the divine principle, whether a god/goddess, nature, creativity, a higher power, or some other form of universal energy.

The sexual arena is also carrying the increased weight of our expectations of our lovers, with whom we want to be transported into realms of bliss. Neo-Tantric approaches to sex in the West are seductive, as they seem to offer an easy way to connect with our romantic partner; their popularity is testament to our need for deeper connection and also spiritual fulfilment.

The tradition of sacred sex

Some seekers think that we can find God through sex, without having to engage in more traditional spiritual disciplines. However, in traditions that used sacred sex, sex was only one part of theological or mystical narratives about divinity and man's place in relation to God or the goddess and the natural world.

Tantric sex had nothing to do with better sex or orgasms. It was sex in the service of a much bigger sense of awareness – a whole-body blissful feeling of being at one with everything that exists, not just with your

In Tantric Buddhism the woman – the skydancer – is necessary to complete/complement the monks' spiritual understanding.

partner but with the entire universe. To paraphrase the early Christians, this was the mystical union, or mystico unio (see also page 26).

Within esoteric traditions in India and Tibet, sex is occasionally used as a sacred rite only after the individual has gone through a lengthy process of spiritual development. Because there is so much potential to use sex in habitual or unconscious ways – which can prove damaging both to self and partner – it is considered a technique for advanced use. Within the Tibetan tradition, typically, adepts would have spent years in meditation, fostering equanimity and compassion in themselves before embarking on practices such as deity yoga (see page 307). Otherwise sex remains just sex, however exotically it is wrapped up in new-age jargon. Creating a spiritual context in which to make love may not change you in any fundamental way but it can change the way you make love!

Relationship expectations

If your relationship is primarily a means of making you feel good about yourself or of meeting your needs for sex, you'll probably end up blaming your partner whenever they are not available to look after you, soothe you or bolster your ego.

Many relationships are damaged by a lack of a healthy sense of self in one or both partners, or by one person's need for control over the other. Sometimes there's a lack of generosity – whether emotionally or materially – or of a shared vision of life. Couples can end up angry and diminished, trapped, distant or in denial about their need for deeper connection, often for years on end.

I've seen many couples expecting sex should be readily available even in such an atmosphere and wondering why it's a disappointing experience. From the perspective of Eastern traditions, you can't embrace sex

We need to learn to negotiate our own boundaries, be more considerate and respect the boundaries of others.

without generating negativity, or bad karma (consequences that become a burden). Thoughtless sex can create more confusion than clarity – and certainly fails to live up to its potential. Our Western culture encourages us to explore sex from a young age, without much forethought, guidance or maturity. We get the message not only that indulging in sex is fine but also that it is our right to be sexually active, even if we are unable to make and sustain loving relationships – so long as we don't actually harm anybody. However, we can see all around us how problematic and potentially hurtful sexuality can be when we behave carelessly. Sex is neither intrinsically good nor bad: what matters is what you do with sexual energy. Sexual self-serving harms ourselves as well as others.

Embarking on the spiritual path

Many people treat the sex drive as if it has its own imperative, which must be satisfied. This can lead to following the genitals rather than the heart, as if the power of this biological force is stronger than your intention. Generations of monks, nuns and ascetics have demonstrated that sex is not necessary for a fulfilling life or for reaching states of mystical experience. Yet some mystical paths in the East harness sexuality and make it part of the practice of meditation, reserving sacred sex for those who are already advanced in their journey to self-realization.

One of the goals of basic training on the spiritual path is to learn meditative techniques that enable you to detach yourself from your urges. Your identity is not defined by survival needs such as thirst, hunger or lust. You are more than your passing moods or behaviours, whether needy, demanding or passive. You are more than your sexuality as well, meaning it need not define you more than you want it to.

The healing power of presence

Presence is a quality of groundedness that makes you feel relaxed, flowing and at ease with yourself. You are aware of your own body and inner processes, as well as the internal state of those around you; your senses are alive; you are alert to the sights, sounds and smells of your environment and enlivened and more receptive to the experiences that life has to offer.

Train yourself to be more present by focusing your attention on your bodily sensations and the sensory experience of your environment regularly throughout the day. Even if it is only for a matter of minutes or seconds, you will immediately feel energized and more present when you do this. Notice the things of fragrance, beauty, pleasure and vitality around you. What you choose to notice cultivates those qualities.

Presence in a relationship

Once you can maintain a steady self-awareness, witnessing your own internal process, it is easier to tune in to other people. Presence, which is an active, focused attention, is the greatest gift you can give someone else. The presence of a mate who is attuned to you emotionally, is sensitive to your needs and can listen and communicate with empathy can be fundamental to letting go of past disappointments, humiliations or abuse and learning to live in the present moment. In the absence of this sort of relationship, many people consult psychotherapists or healers.

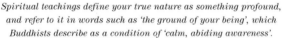

Spiritual teachings define your true nature as something profound,
and refer to it in words such as 'the ground of your being', which
Buddhists describe as a condition of 'calm, abiding awareness'.

In effect, they are paying for presence, a vital precondition for healing relationship wounds.

According to proponents of sacred sex, the relationship itself can bring healing for both parties. The relationship proves its strength as a container – like an alchemical vessel – in which negativity can be separated out from the essential nature of sexuality, getting rid of impurities. If your partner is neither judgemental nor frightened by the knowledge of some of the damaging experiences that may have blighted a healthy sense of self and sexuality, the relationship can transmute into something precious and refined.

Mindfulness

Mindfulness is a type of meditation, and any style is good for stilling the mind and calming the emotions, allowing a quality of presence to emerge. The *Diamond Sutra* says it all: 'Try to develop a mind that does not cling to anything.' Meditation is the first step in the process of learning to let go of your attachment to pain or drama and uncovering 'the ground of

Mindfulness involves centring yourself within your body and allowing your mental processes to settle. This is the first step in meditative exercises.

your being'. Getting a glimpse of a steady and calm quality underneath the practical or emotional dramas of life is often achieved through reflection, meditation or prayer. (See also page 242, The Practice of Presence.) Spiritual teachers remind us that this calm, abiding presence is always available to us, whenever we stop distracting ourselves with entertainment, chatter, thoughts, worries and emotional dramas.

Love as meditation

The mystical dimension uses meditation to open ourselves to the knowledge of divine love or union. The union established during meditation – or prayer – has to be integrated into daily awareness. The spiritual goal of cultivating awareness is for it to become a constant presence in your life, so that you feel rooted in your vital energy – which is the source of both rest and action. The delightful peace tasted in the early stages becomes a normal state, and you can remain in a grounded meditative state even while fully engaged in the world.

Mindfulness is now widely taught in many Western settings. Some decades ago, Jon Kabat-Zinn (1944–) brought mindfulness into the mainstream, drawing from Zen Buddhism, Hatha yoga and other disciplines.

Meditation is a fundamental technique for cultivating the quality of presence – being there for other people. In order to have a good relationship with others, you need to create a good one with yourself. If you can be a witness to your own internal processes, you know how to act as a witness for those of others; and you do not feel that you have to intervene in order to make them feel better. It prevents the need to 'fix' people and empowers them.

The healing power of sexual love

To develop an awareness of sex as sacred is to become aware of the power of sexual energy and use it to deepen connection – not just with your partner, but with your family, neighbours and wider community. It is this fundamental change of attitude that offers potential for healing.

When you are able to honour, trust, communicate, improve your skills as a lover, and focus your mind and body in the appropriate ways, a whole new world of possibilities opens. What is revealed is a capacity for greater understanding, deeper compassion, power, bliss and ecstasy.

Healing the masculine

According to Baba Dez, a self-styled West Coast sexual healer, learning the power of presence is crucial in enabling men to connect more deeply in relationships. He suggests that common patterns such as impatience, distraction, addiction, neglect, exploitation and abuse may be bound up in our culture's pervasive sense of shame; a belief that there's something intrinsically wrong or dirty about sex. This leads to both repression and obsession – two sides of the same coin.

Baba Dez recommends that men explore and amplify their inner feminine (see page 152), becoming more balanced, sensitive and caring. Once a man has achieved this, he can 'hold on to himself', while providing a safe haven for his partner to let go of her defences and be vulnerable, if necessary. Taking the whole process a step closer to sacred sex, if he can embody the divine himself, embodying and emanating both love and awareness, his partner can relax into her own loving flow, getting in touch with her inner divinity.

Healing the feminine

When the inner feminine is weak, there is a tendency to project a feeling of lack outwards onto a partner, and then get angry when those needs are not met, which drives your partner away. This process of putting your needs on someone else is called projection; psychoanalysis has shown that recognizing your own difficult emotions and accepting them is essential to creating a mature and loving relationship.

In order to heal this inner wound you may need to acknowledge the needy, afraid, disconnected part of yourself and nourish yourself, rather than expecting your partner to take care of you. Cultivate a relationship with the feminine part of yourself, the Divine Feminine or the archetype of the Goddess.

The divine goddess is complete in herself and processes all relationships with living things; she tolerates darkness and distance; embrace loves and joy.

Free your emotions

Many of us feel overloaded with toxic emotions – stuff that may belong in the past, or in our own heads, but certainly doesn't belong in the present moment. In order to express emotions freely without identifying with them too closely, think of them as just a form of energy. Strong feelings are a sign of a fluid and responsive attitude to life – but sometimes we give our emotions more weight than they are worth, forgetting that healthy emotions come and go.

It can be a challenge to accept your own emotions and even more of a challenge not to take on someone else's anger or pain. However, you are more likely to be able to help your partner if you can remain relaxed when he or she is emotionally volatile, so that you can listen to what they are trying to communicate.

This helps you learn to be present with one another: you can be both grounded and solid in your sense of self, but without that same sense of self separating you from each other. Whatever is going on between you, practise remaining connected and keeping your heart and mind open to the needs of the moment.

Fostering compassion

According to Buddhist teacher Ajahn Sucitto, feeling intimidated or irritated by other people's behaviour and attempting to hide our shameful negative reactions creates boundaries that separate us from others. Such boundaries ultimately interfere with how we relate to other people.

In becoming more conscious of kindly and compassionate feelings toward others, we can release ourselves from both high expectations and shame or unworthiness. In preventing disappointment and conflict from turning into criticism or complaint about life, we need to stop judging ourselves as well.

A key practice in Buddhism is to cultivate the quality of compassion in order to release negative attitudes that cramp our minds and limit

our receptivity to others. The cultivation of loving-kindness isn't about making yourself imagine that you like or love everyone, but about meeting each moment without preconceptions or emotional resistance.

When you fall in love, everything about you is an outpouring of love. This is the relevance of the Buddhist emphasis on right living. When you are full of love, your thoughts, feelings, speech, and actions all become divine. Appreciating all the love you have in your life keeps you open to love.

Meditation can be done together or solo – what is important is clarity and focus of your presence during meditation.

Exercise:
Creating compassion

The practice of empathy

Compassion is the key to deepening your love and connection to others. Compassion involves empathy – focusing on similarities rather than differences. We all make decisions about how to run our lives based on our desire for happiness. This desire is universal.

1 First, create a calm mood. Sit comfortably and bring your attention to your breath, filling and emptying your lungs. Settle into a slow, gentle rhythm of breathing. Focus on the breath. Feel thankful for your body. Send healing breath into any areas that feel uncomfortable. Sit with this healing breath radiating throughout your body. Notice how your body expands with the loving kindness of your positive intention towards yourself.

2 Relax your body as you imagine releasing negative thoughts with every out-breath. If you feel the slightest disturbance, bring your attention back to your inner calm and notice the parts of your body that feel comfortable, reminding yourself that you are quite okay as you are.

3 Allow well-being to flood your system. Let go of any sense of unease or dissatisfaction. Allow your feelings to be as they are, but do not pay any particular attention to them; investigating them will distract you.

4 Let feelings such as anger, resentment or sadness go, without forcing them.

5 With practice, you can enter this state at will. When you can do this, begin to cultivate this practice whenever you're in the company of others.

Exercise: Co-creating compassion with your partner

Sending out waves of well-being

The more advanced Buddhist practice is to generate loving kindness towards those with whom you have a troubled relationship. The challenge is to learn to hold onto your own well-being, even when your partner is angry or upset. You are more likely to find an appropriate response if you're not feeling agitated yourself.

1 Sit on a cushion on the floor, in a comfortable yoga posture, facing each other, but a couple of feet apart. Start with your eyes closed, while you concentrate on relaxing and deepening your breath.

2 With each in-breath, feel your heart opening like a bud. With each out-breath, send your love outwards toward your lover. Feel the loving connection created as your breath intermingles. As you breathe out, send out the idea of your partner's heart flowering. If you are a word-oriented person, think 'may your heart open with love'. If you are a visual thinker, imagine sending your partner an image of a flower.

3 Notice that your partner's attempts to create happiness are just like your own. Feel compassion for the ways they express their difficulties. They are doing the best they can to find love and happiness, just as you are. Let compassion fill your heart.

4 With every out-breath, send out waves of compassion. With your out-breath, voice or think something like, 'may you find love and happiness'.

5 After several minutes, close the meditation with a warm, melting embrace, maintaining your generous wish for your partner's well-being.

Learning to receive

Sometimes your partner is able to be totally present, yet you find that the impulse arises to draw back. Many couple therapists have commented on this dance of intimacy, in which one person claims to crave closeness with a withholding partner, while in other relationships there appears to be a bit of a see-saw. Once the withholding person moves forward, the other partner unaccountably seems less keen on intimacy. Such patterns may be unconscious, and psychotherapists largely link them to early experiences growing up, with our attempts to deal with insufficient love or over-intrusive parents. According to therapist John Welwood, underneath many people's longing for love lies a deep sense of unworthiness, which can wreak havoc in relationships. This needs to be healed in order to be able to tolerate someone else's

Once you can accept yourself as you are, you become aware that you don't have to prove that you are desirable, interesting or special in order to be loved.

Releasing Self-judgement

Gaze at yourself in the mirror with the eyes of someone who you know loves and trusts you. Someone who thinks you're great – maybe a young child, who hasn't yet learnt to look with critical eyes. The gaze of someone who isn't judging you or noticing any defects, whether real or imagined. Their eyes look at you, and into you, recognizing your good qualities: honesty, loyalty, kindness, your fun side – whatever qualities they appreciate, evoke these same emotions in your heart as you gaze appreciatively at yourself in the mirror.

Focus on allowing the knowledge that you are deeply loved and considered special to enter your awareness, filling yourself with loving feelings.

Become aware that love is all around, and focus on incorporating this into how you see yourself; let it nourish you.

attentive presence or to welcome intimacy. Before being able to receive love from a partner, let alone invite the dimension of the sacred into your relationship, you may need to acknowledge and accept your unworthiness. Accepting the feeling does not mean accepting that your self-belief is valid. Welwood suggests that you soften emotionally whenever that thought comes up – by allowing the feeling to arise and give it some space in your conscious awareness. This technique releases some of the energy that you hold in when trying to contain a difficult feeling. This way you can start to work with it and gradually dissolve it.

Cultivating self-esteem

When someone loves or needs us, this can bolster our sense of self. Many of us see physical affection as evidence that we are loved, ignoring the fact that sex may not be particularly loving or rewarding. It can be hard to let go of an unloving relationship even if it's unsatisfying, because of a fear of being worthless without a partner. Without seeing ourselves as lovable through the eyes of another, we are returned to an underlying sense of unworthiness. Low self-esteem can mean that women, in particular, are overly concerned with trying to keep their men happy and sexually interested, without also making sure they are sexually interested and happy. Without good self-esteem it can be difficult to discuss what you want sexually or to make more radical changes in your sexual style.

Focusing on giving pleasure, rather than exploring it together in a mutually rewarding fashion, can lead to sexual passivity where you expect your partner to bring you to sexual ecstasy. If you are unable to be authentic during sex, you become increasingly dissatisfied. On the other hand, however, you can fear suffocation or the loss of self in merging with your partner. It is a challenge to surrender neediness and fears without losing your sense of self. Learning to be a witness to your own emotions without over-identifying with those of others will help you do just that.

Body negative, body positive

We are bombarded with images of young, thin women who conform to a current stereotype about what it means to be sexy; the less womanly and the more juvenile the better. Sexiness is considered an essential

There is so much more to you – your heart and mind; your sensations, emotions, thoughts and dreams; your compassion or passions; your conscious awareness; your loving nature, your soul.

component of attractiveness: apparently, if you're not sexy, you're just not desirable. Women, in particular, have been sucked into identifying with appearance, while many men believe there is something natural and biologically determined about our culture's obsession with looks rather than friendship and connection.

I don't believe there is a biological basis for what we consider to be sexually attractive. In other cultures and other periods in history there have been quite different standards of beauty to that of our own time. Too many women spend time and money on cosmetics, fashion dieting and exercise rather than on engaging with their own lives and core values in a meaningful way – which is the real way to work at improving damaged self-esteem.

Narcissistic cults of body appearance (rather than throwing yourself into lived experience) leave many people with eating problems, compulsive exercise habits and even body dysmorphia or gender dysphoria, in which the desire to change gender is often over-riding.

Sexual pleasure – solo and together

To be sexual in an abandoned way means being able to be fully present with yourself, to be well disposed towards and accepting of yourself. During self-pleasuring, release your guilt and shame and work on cultivating a positive attitude to your own body and the sensory pleasures it gives you.

It's helpful if your solo sex style is close to how you would like it to be when you're with a lover – otherwise you can habituate yourself to using fantasy or going for maximum genital stimulation rather than immersing yourself in bodily sensations and tuning your awareness to the more sensual and subtle dimensions of your experience. Such poor habits will

The yab-yom posture allows a couple to focus on breathing and moving energy around, while mirroring each other and exchanging energy at the level of genitals, heart, mouth and third eye.

diminish the quality of the sexual exchange you have with a partner. The most important thing is to slow right down and explore your sensuality. It can be easier to explore breathing, the movement of energy and Tantric visualizations during solo sex.

Self-pleasure

You can use self-pleasuring as a time to develop qualities you would like to express with a partner. For instance, some women could practise getting in touch with their direct and dynamic side, while men might benefit from encouraging their sensitive soulful side. Both could practise sensing the movement of energy in their body when sexually aroused, as described in chakra systems. It is this energy that is harnessed in Daoist and Tantric styles of love-making. Men could experiment with delaying orgasm, and see what it would be like to orgasm without ejaculating (see page 252). Both sexes can experiment with relaxing into sensual pleasure, with learning to let arousal ebb and flow while maintaining high levels of excitement. Encouraging erotic feelings to spread through your whole body, and exploring different styles and a pace of touching yourself to keep pleasure intense, while not going for orgasmic release, are useful skills for sacred sex. At the moment of orgasm, you can focus on offering your mini bliss into a larger ocean of bliss.

The possibilities for exploring the sacred side of sex when solo are great. You can also explore Tantric bodywork, breathing and visualization just as if you were with a partner. Within Tibetan Buddhism there is a strong tradition of taking an imaginary lover as a spiritual practice – a skydancer, or dakini, with whom you can practise and refine a spiritual attitude to sex as a gateway to non-duality, should you choose to do so.

Exercise:
Expanding orgasm

Harness the energy within

The key to expanding orgasm from a local genital experience is to become aware of energy. Most Eastern traditions talk about sexual energy being located in the belly or the solar plexus, the powerhouse of your energy. Kundalini yoga locates the source of your life energy – and sexual power – in the area of your genitals before imagining it coursing upwards (with each out-breath), infusing the rest of your body with sexual vitality.

1 First learn to concentrate the energy in your genitals. As your genitals become warm and sensitized, draw the sensual energy upwards and outwards. Use your hands to trace the movement of it upwards.

2 Squeeze your love muscles to spread the energy through your body, stroking the skin upwards with your hands, as you imagine heat or energy moving upwards.

3 Sense the movement of energy within and without you. Use the model of the chakras to help you imagine the movement of sexual heat or energy throughout this system. Sense the energy as heat or light.

4 When you are ready, bring these techniques to bed with your lover. It is crucial to not use techniques drawn from sacred sex traditions as another means of focusing on yourself; you need to be totally present to what is going on for both of you, in a state of open connection, both during and after love-making.

Cultivating relationship

A strong relationship serves as a crucible in which to explore and accept your own sensuality and let it grow, fed by your own loving awareness, which you can choose to share with your partner. The expanded awareness that you create together may then morph into a larger entity.

Couple therapist David Schnarch talks about differentiation (where each partner has the courage to be themselves, even in the face of attempts by lovers to force them to change) as a fundamental requirement for a good relationship. Partners take responsibility for soothing their own troubled emotional states, even when they choose to share these troubles with the other person. They stay true to their core values and priorities, even while making time for togetherness and committing to staying in connection with the other. They find easy ways to stay alive to the demands of a shared life, yet honour differences and negotiate compromises where necessary. When love, trust and the capacity to surrender are all present in a strong relationship, compromise does not involve a diminution of self, but a strengthening. Likewise, supporting each other through tough times feels natural and fulfilling, rather than a sacrifice.

Learning to talk about sex

Sexuality is a way of knowing yourself and your lover. Through your sexual relationship (with yourself and with your lover), you can find out more about who you are and learn to communicate that information in an intimate way. Good communication enables you to express what you

Learning to talk freely about sex and understand each other will intensify your appreciation of sex, and allow you to relax into it while it is happening.

want. You can be clear about your own experiences, what you do and don't like and set clear boundaries on any aspects of sex that make you feel uncomfortable, for whatever reason. With each person taking responsibility for communicating the details of their own sexual process, sex is no longer used as a way of controlling your partner – or manipulating them through withholding – but as a way of enjoying what's good for each of you. You can learn more give and take without continually compromising your desires and limiting your sexual play.

Reigniting sexual fire

Many people complain of diminishing sexual interest as a relationship progresses, and a surprising number of couples cohabit in no-sex relationships. This may occur if couples haven't developed the sexual skills necessary for both parties to feel sexually satisfied – in which case, at least one person usually becomes averse to the mere thought of sex. Going to a good sex therapist is an excellent place to start – and the sooner the better.

Often, sex isn't happening due to unresolved conflict or difficulties in the relationship, or long-standing emotions such as resentment or distrust that continue to get in the way of erotic conversation and connection. Whatever the cause, withdrawing from sex quickly becomes habitual. A lack of affectionate touch or caring expressions of appreciation builds a firm wall that it seems daunting to even approach, let alone attempt to find a way through.

Caress the body

Foot rubs, hand-holding, hugs and simply lying together with any part of your body touching in a non-intrusive or -demanding way while you learn to listen to one another again and talk freely will begin to heal deprivation and re-create physical intimacy. Massage and looking directly at one another, whether you are communicating verbally or non-verbally, are two key ways to deepen intimacy.

You may want to start by sitting on the sofa without making eye contact as you find your way back to the self-disclosure that is a sure sign

While enjoying a foot rub, focus on receiving. Revel in the gift of your partner's care, attention and healing touch.

of trusting intimacy. If you are fully relaxed and comfortable when lying together with full body contact, and are able to gaze into your lover's eyes without feeling self-conscious or embarrassed, you have made it back to connection and are ready to deepen your sexual intimacy. Appreciative, non-demanding, yet intimate physical touch every day will soon re-create a flow of sexual energy.

When you feel complete in yourself and are overflowing with love, sex
can be a crucible for growth and transformation. When two people
who are full of love make love, their sense of distance dissolves.

Using sexuality to connect

Sometimes couples have a very sexual relationship but lack intimacy in other areas. Loving sex activates the chemical pathways leading to release of the bonding chemical oxytocin, sometimes called the cuddling hormone. Having more sex will deepen your relationship – unless the sex is unsatisfying.

Different styles of sex generate different feel-good chemicals. Whereas hot sex activates production of endorphins, which produce the same chemical high we get from a good work-out, phenylethylamine (also found in chocolate) is more associated with the release of dopamine in the pleasure centres of the brain. Loving sex can be used to create a more intimate style of relationship, which gives you access to even deeper love and connection. If you both cultivate a more sensitive sexuality and bring this into your relationship, you can blend beautifully.

Two become one

The more you discover your own sexuality and your partner's sexual process, the more intense your connection becomes. If you have established a sensitive connection, you can bring to the relationship your self-awareness, self-knowing, emotional expression and your empathy, caring and desire to discover ever more about your partner. Your relationship increases in fulfilment.

Our stressful thoughts about ourselves, the undercurrents in our interaction with our lovers and our concerns about how to interpret what is going on during sex are the kinds of worries that prevent us from entering a state of flow and connectedness.

Deepening your awareness

It takes a lot of practice to move from spontaneous glimpses of an all-inclusive Big Mind to holding a vision of reality as a continuous field of consciousness. Regular and often intensive practice to retrain your consciousness is an important feature of spiritual life. Meditation involves cultivating an awareness of reality while still engaged in mundane – and not-so-mundane – activities.

Adepts practise meditation and other techniques to glimpse non-dual awareness (that there is no fundamental difference between self and other, or self and object). Later they work at creating an enduring and constant awareness of non-duality. Enlightenment cannot be forced – but you can prepare for it. Enlightenment is the realization that there is only one mind: our individual mind, with its preoccupations and self-centred awareness, is a drop in the ocean of consciousness.

In Tibetan Buddhism the dakini, or sky-dancer, represents the visionary realm of ritual practice.

Creating a sense of the divine

By reflecting on the nature of reality and fostering a transcendent vision of life, you can develop a much more inclusive perspective. This opens you to enlightenment experiences, no matter how transient – what scholar Huston Smith calls 'transforming flashes of illumination into abiding light'. If you use sex as a way of getting away from your own mind rather than clear it before you have sex, such thoughts will keep intruding. The Tantric idea of establishing a solid practice of meditation before embarking on sacred sex, and treating sex itself as a form of meditation, can help you to enter the flow of love-making. Connecting with your partner in this attitude of presence connects you with reality. Making love as if you are both divine connects sex to the sacred. This is where sex has the potential to open into the realm of bliss, which the Tantras describe as the underlying truth of reality.

- Appreciate that you have this wonderful person in your life.
- Reaffirm love on a daily basis – it needs constant nurture.
- Cultivate presence – learn to really be there for your partner.
- See your partner as a god or goddess.
- Express your own divine
- Cultivate bliss.

Rethinking sexual satisfaction

Deepening sex means widening your definition of sex. Great sex involves far more than two bodies having intercourse with the

ultimate aim of achieving orgasm for both partners. The fact that so many couples lose interest in sex or find it boring is testament to the unsexiness and limitations of this functional model of sex.

If our frame of mind largely determines how we experience sex, our compartmentalized thoughts about sex may be blocking us from experiencing sex as so much more.

Consider orgasm, as an example: there is far more to orgasm than genital stimulation and the release of muscle spasms, however enjoyable. Below, I have listed just some of the many ways couples describe their experiences.

Making sex more engaging and meaningful may require deepening the qualities in your relationship rather than focusing on increasing desire and genital arousal. After all, if sex is satisfying in a deeper way, you'll want to indulge in more of it. Satisfying sex is more of a whole-person process for both individuals – one that creates connections among body, mind, heart and soul.

Types of orgasm

Orgasm is usually defined as a liberating discharge and release of sexual tension after a period of strenuous genital stimulation – which, in most people's minds, boils down to intercourse. New York sex educator Betty Dodson pioneered programmes teaching women who had not had orgasms before. Inspired by her work, I've listed some of my favourites:

Multiple orgasm
Sexual stimulation is continued until orgasms occur again and again.

Extended orgasm
Extending a single orgasm into a lengthy one with peaks and troughs of pleasure. One method is to alternate between pleasuring different erogenous zones – for example, g-spot and clitoris for women, penis and perineal area for men, as in Bauer's guide, *Extended Sexual Orgasm*.

Non-ejaculatory orgasm
Genital release is controlled in order to redirect sexual energy or to keep it within the body, rather than dissipating it through ejaculation.

Making Sex Sacred: Practical Pathways to Bliss

According to early research by maverick consciousness researcher John Lilly, the parts of the brain that control erection, orgasm and ejaculation are located in separate areas of the brain – and these pathways are integrated elsewhere. So for men, orgasm and ejaculation can be triggered separately, just as Mantak Chia teaches in The *Multi-orgasmic Man*.

The valley orgasm
This occurs when you totally relax into love-making rather than tensing your muscles to build arousal. Fully present, you surrender to pleasure.

Whole-body orgasm
Most people describe this as waves of energy flooding the body starting from the genital area, rather than the local genital muscular spasms associated with regular orgasm.

Oceanic sex
Psychiatrist Stanislav Grof described oceanic sex as a playful flow and exchange of energies resembling a dance. The dance involves losing body boundaries, while melting with the partner.

The energy orgasm
The body is one energy field, and when people are making love these energy fields inter-penetrate each other. Whereas Indian models often describe seven energy centres, or chakras, in the body, Daoist instructor Mantak Chia describes three: in the area of navel, heart and head. Circulating these energies throughout your joined bodies, an orgasm may occur when you relax into the energy flow located at the energy centres.

Kundalini orgasm

A yoga practice in which energy moves up from the pelvis through the energy channels in the centre of the body and flows out of the top of the head (vertex).

Tantric orgasm

Genital union is the path toward the ultimate goal of transcendental union of the male and female principles in the 'big O' of oneness, creating bliss. In Tantra, the whole world is considered sexual in essence.

Thought orgasms

No-hands orgasms where the imagination does all the work – sometimes using PC pumps to squeeze the love muscles using movement and breath.

Heart orgasms

Where your heart is full of love and overflows into melting pleasure.

Bliss

Where the nature of the universe is revealed. These experiences may relate to bliss as described in the Eastern Tantras, or a pulsating field of energy, or other form of consciousness.

Getting beyond orgasm

In some ways it is hard not to connect when making love. Western culture encourages us to separate sex from the wider context of the relationship, divorcing sex from love and encouraging each individual to go for self-gratification, while acknowledging that it's nice if our partner 'comes' too. Conventional sex therapy exacerbates this tendency to disconnect by encouraging individuals to disappear inside their own head and fantasize in order to increase arousal.

This leads to sexual dissatisfaction, because eroticism involves far more than two bodies engaged in functional sex; it grows in the connections created between two people – and in emotions such as love, compassion, altruism, empathy and awe. All these extra dimensions contribute to make sexual arousal extraordinary and meaningful. You can develop these qualities in love-making simply by paying attention to them.

Togetherness

Sink into your own experience, enjoying the sensuality and relaxing into togetherness rather than focusing on genital pleasure. Focus on encouraging erotic energy to permeate your whole body and stream out of your body, into that of your lover.

If you are a visual person, imagine a rainbow of colours streaming from your own body into your lover's, while embracing or when making love. Imagine the pair of you enveloped in a cocoon of warm bright light. Let your positive emotions enliven this energy body, as you fill the cocoon with the quality of love.

Deeply sharing your warm loving feelings can be more sexy than having sex.

Exercise: Non-doing
in sex – the 'soul' orgasm

Letting go of the idea of performance

The soul orgasm arises out of an experience of being, rather than doing; of merging, not 'being done to' or 'doing to' your partner. It's about total relaxation rather than performance. The body registers such an experience as profoundly bonding, unlike the performance-oriented genital orgasm or even the whole-body orgasm. You are deeply connected but without expectations or intent, open to whatever you create together.

1 Lie with your partner, just feeling their presence and then expressing this through gentle touch. Eventually you will find that you don't need to do anything to stay connected.

2 A tendency is to try to create more excitement through more and more stimulation, doing things in different ways or trying out kinky activities. Instead, be sensitive to what is there – fully experiencing your sensations. Feel the powerful sensation of slow, delicate touch on your skin.

3 Slow down, breathe and maintain eye contact, so that you feel closely connected with each other. It's important not to tense your muscles as you do in trying to make something happen.

4 Breathe into your heart centre and soften your awareness. Alternate this total relaxation by squeezing your love muscle, or use a gentle stroking for a pleasurable sensation over the body. Explore non-doing even when you choose to have intercourse. Penetration is often soft penetration. The woman guides her partner's soft penis inside – without him worrying if his erection is firm.

5 Enjoy the gentle healing contact between your genitals rather than pursuing vigorous contact. It can be just as exciting.

Sex as energy

Embrace sex for the sheer joy of pleasurable eroticism, rather than with any particular script or agenda. Experience sex as a meeting of two energies and enter the flow; respond to your partner, in the present. Moment to moment, simply follow your heart, feel playful and inspired, deeply relax, or melt into the embrace of your lover. Treat any emotions that arise during sex as different manifestations of the same energy flow – go with them. When you embrace desire as an energy, rather than focusing on any predefined goal, you can relax and enjoy sex without worrying about where you're going.

Thinking about sex in this way may help you not to either clutch on to transient pleasures – no matter how lovely – or get distracted by momentary irritational emotions or negativity. It can be good to talk about all of these things after-wards, and share with your partner your own experience, putting into words how you experienced the dance of energy. This is a bit

Dance and music can take you into deeper presence, if you let the music flow through you, and the dance to transport your body.

different from the usual query of 'how was it for you, darling?', which is all too often focused on the quality of your orgasm, if any. Experiment with treating the connection between the two of you as one of energy. Visualize your passion as heat and let it enliven your body. Experience yourself as dynamic and sexy. Let your sexual charge build and instead of rushing to dissipate it, stay with it, letting the erotic power build more and more as you remain intensely present with your partner, engaging fully in your love play. Imagine yourself offering that erotic energy to your partner, for them to enjoy and bask in its heat. Feel them receiving your sexual force, incorporating it to charge their own body. Enjoy their potency without feeling intimidated, and keep your own vitality strong, meeting them with equal intensity. Enjoy this dance of energy as your energy fields merge and mutate. Let your energy bodies dance together.

The three keys to better sex

According to sexual ecstasy teacher Margot Anand, a key figure in introducing Tantra to the West, there are three keys to better sex. Breath, movement and sound all allow you to enter your sensual experience more deeply and increase pleasure.

• During deep breathing, relax your whole body at the same time as it is feeling invigorated by the increased oxygen supply. Breathing enables you to experience your body sensations more intensely.

• Relax into your body and your physical experience so that tight muscles and blocked energy do not stop pleasure from moving through your body.

• Use sighs and other sounds to clearly express your sensual pleasure – and communicate it to your partner. Breath, movement and sound all allow you to feel sensations more strongly.

Exercise: Creating more love

Appreciation

Reminding yourself daily of all the good in your partner, and the positive dimensions he or she adds to your life, is a wonderful meditation. This practice is more positive than focusing on any deficits you may perceive. The more you respond enthusiastically to the great things about them, the more likely they are to carry on behaving in a loving way,

1 Praise your partner for all the kind and thoughtful things they do for you and the family, and others.

2 Acknowledge how important they are to you.

3 Demonstrate in words, looks, touch and loving messages, your appreciation.

4 Find ways of doing small services for them – whether it's a cup of tea, a foot massage, or a loving note.

5 Learn to listen to what they are trying to communicate underneath the familiar words they are speaking.

6 Open your heart and feel empathy, compassion and love towards your mate.

7 Focus on loving feelings filling your heart as you gaze at your partner. Find words to express your love – whether in compliments, letters, poetry or music.

8 Think about all the fabulous qualities your partner has whenever they're not around, and tell others about them, instead of complaining. Give your partner your full attention when they speak. The gift of presence is priceless.

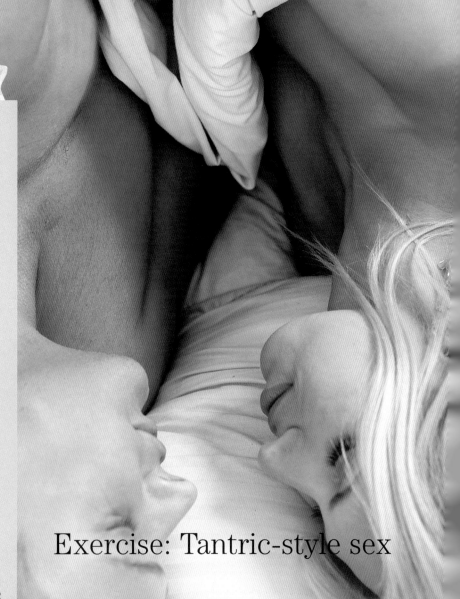

Exercise: Tantric-style sex

Deepen your pleasure

Use intimacy, trust and relaxation to develop your erotic potential. Your sexual passion builds up energy that can be channelled into rapture. Using meditation and visualization techniques to arouse your senses during love-making helps you to fully enter your bodily experience.

1 As your lover strokes your face and hair, focus fully on his or her touch. When your lover's hand caresses your flesh, melt into that delicious sensory awareness. When your lover kisses you all over, feel their loving intent and their love permeate your body.

2 Connect with your partner's heart centre, through exchanging breath or a loving gaze, or visualizing the movement of energy between the two hearts.

3 As your lover embraces you, imagine that you are both held in a warm cocoon of love. Inhale the sweet breath of your lover, nourishing your own life force. When aroused, focus on your breathing; breathe slowly and deeply to deepen your arousal.

4 As your lover plays with your genitals, encourage the erotic fire to keep building in your pelvis. Gently and rhythmically squeeze the muscles around your genitals to increase sexual heat.

5 As your excitement mounts, focus on drawing your energy from your genitals up your spine (through the central energy channel) to your heart chakra, up to your brow.

6 As your genitals come together, allow your sexual pleasure to pervade your heart, and fill you with joy.

7 During love-making, draw the sexual energy from your heart up to the energy centre at the crown of your head, creating bliss.

Opening your heart

Love is simply when you open your heart. In love, you allow yourself to relax into the love between you, so that you become one with whomever or whatever you are contemplating, whether a child, a lover or nature.

Openness means meeting the moment without resistance. Allow the connection between the two of you to be as it is, without tensing up or withholding your own emotional contact. Allow your partner to get closer to you, without withdrawing or hiding your vulnerability. Enjoy being seen by your partner. Love involves connecting in an atmosphere of unity that tolerates and absorbs difference. There is no limit to love – you can love every person and every thing in the world.

The more you love,
the more love increases.

Recognizing the Connection

You'll know when loving sex is connecting you with
your self and your beloved when:

You feel more alive.

You feel more authentic – totally yourself.

You feel more loving.

Love is already a part of you.

You love and accept yourself more and accept others
just as they are.

You meet in the present moment rather than comparing
this meeting with any other.

You abandon judgement, separation, division or alienation.

You abandon clinging and neediness.

You discover that we are all one and that you don't need to try
to connect because you already are connected. We all have the
same fundamental needs for acceptance, love and connection.

You can love yourself, your partner, your life and the whole
of life without a sense of separation.

You stop thinking about sex during love-making. Making love
is more about connecting than techniques.

Exercise:
Open your heart visualization

Connect sex and heart centres

Eastern sacred sex practices involve bringing sexual energy into your heart area in order to infuse it with love. This is important before approaching your partner sexually.

1 Using the chakra model of the energy body, imagine your sexual energy spreading upwards from your pelvis and into the area of your heart, where you concentrate on infusing it with love.

2 With every in-breath, imagine drawing up the sexual energy through your body, to your heart.

3 Use your hand to gesture on the outside of your body, so that your partner knows roughly what you're visualizing at any given moment.

4 Generate loving feelings in your heart and let the power of your erotic energy increase this lovingness even more. Exchange energy between the two of you at the level of your heart, becoming aware of the differences between giving, receiving and merging.

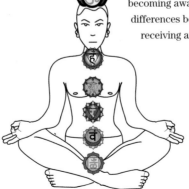

347

Sexual brain training

Scientific research suggests that consciously directing your energy in states of meditation has measurable effects. Brain scans show thoughts as electrical signals, and scans of meditating Tibetan monks show circuits being activated in the brain. It is now accepted that the brain is extremely plastic. Our sex drive and patterns for emotional attachment and sexual arousal are not hard-wired. We can train ourselves to create the kind of associations and responses that we wish to. It doesn't matter whether you agree with the objective existence of things like chakras – what is relevant is your subjective experience. Neuroscience also shows that focusing your attention – as in meditation or visualization – creates the same kind of neurological circuits as actually doing those things. So practising new skills in visualization and meditation will give you a head

Yoga trains your body to respond to the new information you are giving it – creating new habits.

start in actualizing these skills in your relationship. It seems that if you direct your awareness by visualizing a circuit through your body, you actively create this circuit. Master practitioners believe that, with practice, these channels become stronger and you can control them, creating a new context for your experience and new responses. These can replace previous response patterns that are no longer helpful.

The Tibetan monk experiment

In a ground-breaking study conducted by Professor Davidson at the University of Wisconsin, the brains of Tibetan Buddhist monks were shown to have much greater activation in neural networks that process empathy and maternal love, and stronger wiring along the neural pathways by which higher thought controls emotions.

Meditation, particularly compassion meditation, produces strong gamma waves, which scientists believe are a signature of neuronal activity that knits together multiple circuits – a neuroscientist's definition of consciousness. Gamma waves appear when the brain brings together multisensory features of an object and the associations that lead to moments of revelation. During compassion meditation, the brains of all the subjects showed activity in regions that monitor emotions, plan and generate happiness. Brain regions that compartmentalize awareness into self and other became quieter, as if during compassion meditation the subjects became identified with others. Experienced monks, who had meditated for at least 10,000 hours, continued to produce strong gamma waves even when they were not meditating. Their brains were different from the brains of novices, and were marked by waves associated with perception, problem solving and higher consciousness.

Accessing sexual ecstasy: channelling energy

The Tantric tradition teaches specific well-trodden pathways for using sexual energy to access ecstatic sexual experiences. The findings of neuroscience suggest that there may be many different styles of consciousness, depending on what we focus on and how we wire our brains. During meditations, visualization seems to stimulate areas of the brain that process sexual and 'spiritual' pleasure to produce what practitioners describe as bliss. Even sceptics report that following Tantric exercises with the help of an experienced partner or teacher will produce profound states as compared with 'normal' sex.

Tantric exercises describe complex circuits within the body that channel energy through different centres (chakras) on the body. Many practices use visualization to direct breath and sexual energy through these chakras (see page 347).

Creating a foundation for sacred sex

Research suggests that through visualizing subtle anatomy, you can actively create such energy circuits. In the language of the neuroscientist, you are mapping them onto your brain through the techniques of visualization and meditation.

Although practitioners have made detailed maps of our bodies' subtle anatomy as if it is as predictable as our physical anatomy, each school has their own variation for instance, some systems describe a different number of chakras. Therefore if you want to experiment with meditations drawn from the Eastern tradition I suggest that you feel free to use whichever system or exercises appeal to you, without worrying about the exact location of any energy wheels or channels of energy, or whether you are using the right colour, gesture or sound in your meditation. These are all aids that are recommended because they've been found to be helpful to practitioners.

Many of the modern Tantra courses guide individuals toward the goal of sexual ecstasy and also use techniques from contemporary psychotherapy practice because of the emotional and communication issues discussed earlier. The exercises suggested in this section are drawn from neo-Tantra.

What Tantra brings to Western sexuality

In our imagination, Tantric sex refers to slow, mindful sexual union – and according to the popular press, it's about lasting hours without ejaculating. In fact, traditional Tantric exercises are more about using sex in a less personalized way – as a meditative practice in which you first need to let go of your unevolved attitudes toward sex. In other words, it's

Make your love-making very different from your normal style – focus on your breathing, meeting your partner afresh in the moment, and flowing together.

How to Change the Context of Sex

Experience sex as a coming together of physical bodies, emotions and energy bodies.

See your partner as an energy body
(sidestepping irritating personality traits).

See your partner as divine (recognizing the divinity in us all).

Use the yoga techniques of breathing, movement and visualization.

Leave your problems and power struggles at the bedroom door.

meditation that just happens to use sex, because of the innate power of the sexual experience to open our eyes to transcendence. Our idea of love and sex within a loving relationship may simply be too small to allow us to understand what Tantra is all about. If we assume our partner is the cause of our sexual excitement and pleasure, then we fear that without them we would lose touch with love. We feel that we need to make love in order to feel this intensity. As long as you think of sex as the bond that connects you and your partner, whenever your connection is weakened for any reason, it may be difficult to access warm loving or blissful feelings.

The art of Tantra is about learning to generate those feelings of bliss in yourself. Developing and deepening your own sexual experience is your responsibility. Once you understand that you are the source of your own blissful feelings, sex becomes a doorway to experiencing your true nature.

Exercise:
Generating
sexual energy

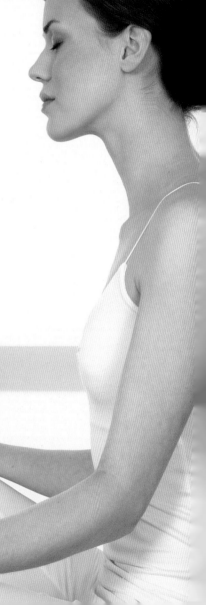

Using your love muscles

When your love muscles are strong, genital sensation and orgasmic pleasure is improved for both men and women. Since the physical strength of your orgasm largely depends on the tone of your pelvic muscles (known as the love muscles), if you have good muscle tone you can pump these muscles to increase sensations during arousal and intercourse. They also increase the power of your sexual energy, intensifying your erotic connection and helping you direct the dynamic energy through your body.

1 Sit in a relaxed pose with your legs crossed loosely, hands resting on the thighs. Focus on your sex – the area of the perineum for men and the vaginal area for women.

2 As you breathe in, pull up your love muscles (pelvic floor muscles). Hold your breath as the erotic energy ascends your spine toward the middle of your forehead.

3 While holding your breath, release and squeeze the pelvic floor muscles about ten times, slowly pumping your love muscle. Release your breath, exhaling through the nose.

4 For the next few breaths, concentrate on drawing the force from the energized area of your sex up through the core of your being. Let it permeate and nourish your energy body.

5 You can pump these love muscles in your lover's arms. Take it in turns to send loving energy toward each other, with each outbreath, once you are warm with the heat of passion.

Step into the energy body

Visualize yourself as an erotic red goddess
Symbol of dedication and passion,
three eyes blazing with passion;
Your tongue is lustful, with the purifying power of your inner fire.
You are a naked goddess with dishevelled hair;
Symbolizing freedom from the bonds of delusion.
You are intuition – a reminder that everything must pass.
Blazing like a fire, you express your wisdom essence,
In embracing your lover without restraint.

From the *Chakra Sambhara Tantra*

Tasting the body as an energy body can transform the experience of self.
Your body is more than your physical structure – it's your body, your mind
and emotions all woven into a whole. Tantric traditions see the body as
interpenetrated by an energy field. When you wake in the morning
visualize your body as a field of energy vibrating gently.

Alternatively, move into a more active form of meditation such as yoga,
stretching, walking or something more dynamic. Power your body through
exercise, movement or dance, enjoying the sense of flow as you fully
inhabit your body. If you feel in flow while swimming, make that a regular
practice. If you feel most in harmony while walking in nature, make sure
to take time outdoors regularly. If dance moves you, put your favourite
music on and abandon yourself to it. Let the music dance you, rather than
trying to dance. Abandon self-consciousness about using your body.

Getting into the flow

In 'flow' you feel fully immersed in whatever you are focused on; your attitude is positive and you are energized. Your awareness and actions are channelled into a congruent sense of engagement. You can't force flow, but dancers, performers and athletes describe it as the product of throwing yourself into something whole-heartedly. This concept of flow is another way of describing realization of your true nature, which arises spontaneously. According to psychologist Mihaly Csíkszentmihályi, intense flow produces joy and bliss.

Use a physical activity that you enjoy to get into the flow; this might be taking a run before you make time together or dancing around the living room.

If yoga and meditation induce a state of flow in you, enhance this state with breath work and visualizations. This is important preparation for enlightenment.

Let the music inspire you to move.
Let the dance take you over.

Exercise: Awakening the senses and the imagination

Nourish the senses

When a person is very much in love, they radiate love and often become inspired and inspiring. Love intensifies their personal presence, whether fiery and passionate or light and loving.

You can hear the voice of love speak through them, see the movement of love in their bodies, and sometimes smell the fragrance of the beloved upon them. This exercise offers suggestions to attune the senses of lovers, although you can come up with many more ideas.

Develop multiple layers of sensory stimulation to enchant your senses in a whole-body approach to sex. When you are with your lover, play with scent, sound, touch, taste, sight and delight in each of these in turn.

Scent

Close your eyes and smell your lover. Inhale their body scent. Smell the nape of their neck, between the breasts, the small of their back, their belly and thighs. Like an animal with a delicate nose, forage those parts of your lover's body that give off strong scents, enjoying them. Your lover's body emits pheromones and their particular scent is what turns you on.

After a bath, use different essential oils or perfumes to anoint your partner's body and discover how it changes their natural scent. Anoint the back of their ears, the nape of the neck, the hollows of the shoulders, the base of the spine.

Inhale their odour deeply, allowing the experience to nourish your awareness of your lover's physicality.

While being smelled, imagine your partner is inhaling parts of your body – your atoms are entering their body via the nose. You are becoming part of them.

Sound

Tune into the sounds around you – the silence, the birdsong, the music. Notice what sounds relax you and help you enter flow. Let the sounds enter you. Tune into the sound of your own breath and your partner's breath, and how they mingle.

Touch

Notice physical sensations anywhere in your body – the feeling of pressure of the objectives that you're touching, and how your body constantly moves and adjusts itself. Enjoy this subtle exchange between your body and the environment. Become more aware of your skin and they way it experiences things. When your partner touches your skin, sense their hand touching you at the same time as your skin receives and appreciates their touch.

Taste

A way of delighting the senses is to bring a tray of food and drink to a bedside table and offer individual items as a taste sensation to your blindfolded partner, choosing flavours and textures that are interesting, intriguing, but not shocking, as your partner needs to feel safe and relaxed in order to take in unseen substances .... Little slivers of kiwi fruit, Indian sweets, crystallized ginger, molten chocolate, avocado, celery – be inventive. Your partner will experience these in a different way without the usual visual clues that make up taste.

Sight

To stimulate the sense of sight, simply remove your partner's blindfold after giving them half an hour of sensory pleasure. If the room is lit with a candle, a soft light will be cast over all the objects you have used to delight and stimulate your partner's senses.

Seeing the body as energy

When your bodies embrace, your two energy bodies meet and become one. Energy is flowing from you through your partner and back to you. Energy is cycling around your system. In my book *Tantric Sex* I describe exercises to cycle the energy through your body in yab-yom (literally

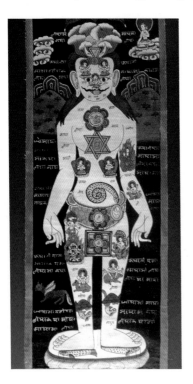

mother-father) position, with genitals and mouth connected.

In the kundalini yoga tradition, the way energy circulates through the system is seen as a magnetic attraction between male and female, which we experience as a sexual attraction. This is rather like the plus and minus poles of an electrical circuit, where opposite charges attract and connect to create a channel through which energy flows. We can use Tantra to really intensify the charge.

Visualize your body as having a subtle anatomy of energy pathways (as in the acupuncture model) and imagine taking the breath down to the genitals and then back up to the heart area on out-breath.

Tantric rituals join principles of feminine and masculine, action and being, compassion and wisdom, immanence and transcendence.

Exercise: Radiant energy meditation

Seeing the light

In this exercise you and your partner see yourselves as radiant beings surrounded in a rainbow of light, linked to the divine.

1 Sit cross-legged on the floor (facing each other if you are doing this exercise with your partner). Then close your eyes and let your breath find a slow, steady rhythm. If your partner's breathing is audible, your breathing should synchronize.

2 Once you have created a tranquil mood, add visual imagery to intensify the meditation. Visualize opening the crown centre at the top of your head, the gateway to the transpersonal realm.

3 Each of you imagine the light streaming in through the crown of your head. Each time you breathe in, imagine drawing this energy down through your body to your belly. As the energy fills your pelvis, hold your breath for a moment, allowing it to permeate your being. Try to imagine this stream of white light expanding out to fill your whole being, illuminating your body so that it becomes a radiant energy body.

4 Release your breath slowly, while your energy body remains illuminated by your breath.

5 If you want to go deeper into the meditation, focus on the sexual energy in your genitals, allowing the white light to concentrate there. Imagine that you are drawing this golden light from your genitals and pelvis with your breath, along the column through the centre of your body. As it moves up toward the crown of your head again, imagine this golden light flooding the energy centres located at your heart, your throat and your brow (third eye). Visualize the light streaming out of your crown to merge with the light streaming out of your partner's head.

Breath and the spirit

In many esoteric systems, the breath has been associated with the spirit. Breathing exercises have been used by different traditions to affect the soul. Among Sufis, the word roh refers to both soul and breath. Among Hindus, prana refers to both; the art of using breath to activate the subtle energy body has been refined into the art of pranayama.

Since many of us breathe shallowly, mostly due to chronic stress or anxiety, it may be helpful to follow a daily meditation practice focusing on the breath. The simplest yoga practice is to concentrate on expelling air through your nose more forcefully, emptying your lungs. The in-breath then takes care of itself, and the lungs fill more deeply. Filling the breath slowly and deeply and then holding the breath for a few seconds also helps to deepen and lengthen breathing. If you aren't interested in breathing exercises, a daily bout of aerobic exercise such as swimming or a vigorous walk will be helpful. During mindfulness practice, you can concentrate on your breath in order to detach from your thoughts and sink into your body (see The Practice of Presence, page 242).

Kundalini energy

During yoga exercises the breath is directed through the various energy conduits of the subtle body, where it moves energy around as it passes. Meditation practices use visualization to imagine where to send the energy (see Tantra chakra visualization on page 347, for example). In the area of your heart, you can gesture towards your partner as you imagine offering your love to them.

Breath is the essence of being human – and in many languages the word also means spirit. Focusing on breathing techniques is also a key part of Tantric exercises.

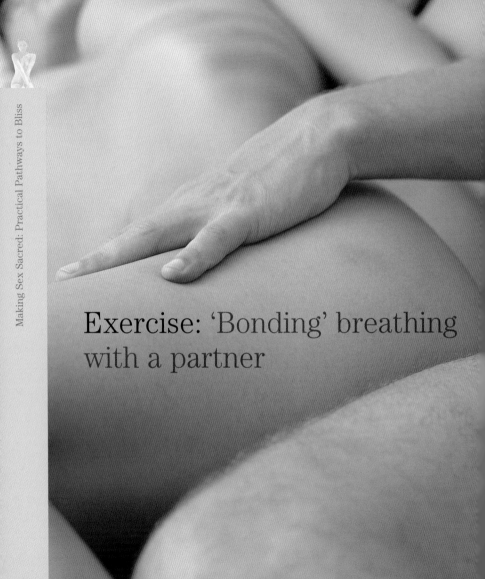

Exercise: 'Bonding' breathing with a partner

Harmonize your breathing

To prepare for an exchange of energies with your partner in Tantra-inspired rituals, focus on the exchange and movement of energy in your body. Once you have got the hang of this, you can practise sitting in front of your partner while you both imagine the same thing together. Practise the exercise with your eyes closed at first. It will help you to pay attention to your internal processes, without immediately trying to synchronize your visualization with that of your partner.

1 Practise imagining your breath travelling down from your mouth to your genital area with every in-breath, and then travelling back up through the centre of your body on every out-breath.

2 Harmonize your breathing so that you are both breathing in and out together, this can be both relaxing and bonding. It works well to do this when you are lying in bed together on your sides and facing the same way. Your partner's breathing should be audible and the person with the faster breathing should slow their breathing down to meet the pace of their partner's.

3 Try a neo-Tantra version of this exercise. Neo-tantra exercises use alternate breathing, where one person breathes in at the same time as their partner breathes out, to prepare for an exchange of energies in exercises like Riding the Wave of Bliss, page 385.

Cultivating sexual chemistry

We regard chemistry as essential to a successful love relationship, yet we usually assume that it is totally outside our control. It remains a mystery why we experience it with some people and not others.

Psychologists have a lot to say about the unconscious factors that underlie attraction and the reasons why couples pair up. But sacred sex is

If your lover is a woman, she manifests the goddess Shakti who, like any goddess, is considered a being of pure energy and compassionate love.

more concerned with developing control of chemistry, so that you can choose where and when to direct it. Sacred sex relies on chemistry to generate sexual energy. Just as we have seen with qualities like compassion and loving kindness, you can cultivate chemistry by becoming aware of it arising in everyday life and focusing on it.

As you are starting to develop it, whenever there's someone around that you find attractive, enjoy your attraction and encourage it to increase rather than suppressing the energy. Own it as yours! You don't need to feel guilty – it doesn't mean that you are going to be unfaithful. The energy belongs to you and doesn't really have much to do with the person who inspires the feeling in you.

The more you focus on it, especially when there is no one else around to stimulate it, the more you can call it up when you want to enrich yourself with it.

Whenever you are with your lover, encourage this chemistry and do the things that increase it. Focus on the social chemistry between you when you want to make love. Use it to let attraction build in your energy body, bringing you into contact with your partner's body.

Venerate your lover as a goddess

The loss of humanity's enduring tradition of goddess worship in the last couple of millennia has left men without a model for viewing women as fit to be worshipped. In treating women as sexual objects or domestic partners, instead of as inherently sacred, men miss out on a whole level of self-awareness. In worshipping a woman, you bring out the best in her, as well as acknowledging your own divine nature.

Exercise: Body of light

Imagine yourself as a body of light

This meditation is inspired by kundalini yoga. As a regular exercise it can help you generally to achieve a peaceful state of mind. Adepts practise it in preparation for a state of awakening (samadhi).

1 Sit calmly and purify your mind and heart of thoughts and desires. Feel your body soften and lighten, becoming insubstantial. Your body is composed of space, with oscillating waves of energy. Feel your body light and full of radiant energy.

2 As you enter a state of meditation, sense the life force gathering at the base of your spine. As it intensifies, feel the life force gradually rise up your spine into your belly, and from there into your heart and then your forehead.

3 When you feel all this potent life force has gathered in your forehead, direct it outwards from your forehead and imagine your body becoming an ethereal body composed of light and energy.

4 Picture the body of light becoming dense and expanding to fill every space in your whole body. Fill your body with light, love and devotion until you become light and love. Let love fill your being.

5 Sit for up to half an hour while you enjoy experiencing yourself as a body of (loving) light.

Venerating the genitals

In countless small shrines throughout India, the lingam, or phallus, sculpted within the female yoni as an emblem of the sacred marriage, is worshipped with garlands of flowers and libations that flow from the lingam over the female genitals and into the earth.

In the same way that the body is treated as a temple, the genitals are treated as sacred. There are rituals for venerating and anointing both male and female genitals.

During love-making, a man can treat his penis as a sacred object through which he shares his love and light. His whole body becomes a tool for creating love and bliss. A woman's vagina and uterus comprise her sacred space – in earlier cultures they were seen as a temple. In accordance with the sanctity of temples, no one should enter without due respect and reverence.

The sanctity of sexuality

Having a sense of the sanctity of your genitals also means you have the confidence to discontinue genital contact whenever it doesn't feel right to you. Many people want their lover to be totally present and engaged in the experience of making love, which they cannot be if they are lost in fantasy or their own private thoughts.

According to the woman-centredness of neo-Tantra, it is up to the woman to determine when and how she wishes to receive a man's penis, and whether she wishes to receive his ejaculate at all. For men, the challenge is to find a more sensitive and receptive sexual style, following

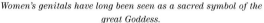

Women's genitals have long been seen as a sacred symbol of the great Goddess.

the woman's leads. Men are also encouraged to discover the ways that holding ejaculation back leaves space for something more profound. In neo-Tantra there is an emphasis on allowing women to determine the style and pace of love-making. Next time you get naked together, maybe after a bath, spend some time appreciating your partner's genitals in a relaxed way – with loving massage or reverent (rather than sexual) caresses. Be gentle and remember when talking about sex and when doing sex, to practise presence, and to call upon the divine goddess.

Exercise:
Venerate the goddess

Inhabit your body as a god or goddess

Manifest your own divine qualities in order to recognize your partner as divine, and meet her at the level of the sacred couple, where love-making sustains the world. The Tantric idea of venerating your partner as a manifestation of the divine is fundamental to accessing bliss. Treat your partner as if she were a goddess and enter love-making as if you were her divine consort. If your lover is a man, treat him as a manifestation of Shiva, your beloved consort.

1 Gaze at your lover with devotion. Glancing is important to chemistry, where you catch the eye of your beloved exchanging understanding and reconnecting, caressing them with your gaze.

2 Let your heart overflow with loving. Your hearts open to each other.

3 View your partner not as a sex object but as a goddess. Treating your partner as precious and sacred means that you relate to what is best in her, and in so doing, identify with what is best in yourself.

4 As you feel your sexual desire rising, look at her with adoration rather than lust.

5 Make your touch respectful and reverential.

6 Honour her with your whole body.

7 Think of entering her body as being as sacred as entering a sacred space.

Homosexuality in Tantra

Respected Buddhist Jeffrey Hopkins adapted his 1992 book *Tibetan Arts of Love* for a gay audience in 1998 as *Sex, Orgasm, and the Mind of Clear Light*, citing Buddhism as sex positive in spite of its resolutely heterosexual orientation, while Christa Schulte has written a guide on neo-Tantra for lesbian and bisexual women.

While Tantric texts and practices are usually based on the heterosex of the divine couple Shakti and Shiva, in other depictions the divine couple are represented as a hermaphrodite to indicate the possibility of uniting the feminine and masculine principles within oneself. Tantric practices often emphasize the polarities of male and female, rather like the positive and negative electrical charges of electrons and protons that hold atoms in molecular relationship. The opposing but intense forces of attraction are similar to those of sub-atomic particles. Tantra refers to this model of the chemistry of sexual attraction to transform subtle energies – connecting the charged energy within and between lovers.

Male and female energy centres

In neo-Tantra, different energy centres are described as masculine and feminine, in order to explain energy transmission. While the emphasis on male and female genitals fitting together can be off-putting for same-sex lovers, what is important is the energy flow between lovers rather than the details of particular energy maps transferred to the physical body. After all, energy maps do not refer to anything fixed or verifiable, but have differing interpretations according to different Tantric traditions.

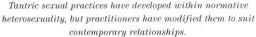

Tantric sexual practices have developed within normative heterosexuality, but practitioners have modified them to suit contemporary relationships.

Tantric practices and rituals have been developed over millennia, in social and cultural contexts that often bear little relation to our own, and you can only ascertain whether they are helpful to you by testing them against your own personal experience. Tantric traditions tend to set personal experience above received knowledge or participation in set rituals. Therefore, these traditions are neither fixed nor immovable; they can be as fluid and flexible as your own enquiry will allow. An important principle in neo-Tantra is opening to divine energy and letting that be your guide to love-making, in the moment.

The yoga of union

Academic Miranda Shaw describes Tantric union as an offering by the man to his sexual partner, using his admiration and respect, the pleasure his body brings her, the sexual fluids he mixes with hers, the breath he mingles, and the subtle energies he exchanges and circulates between them as offerings to her divine nature. Love-making is the ultimate act of worship.

In the yoga of union, sex is an offering to the spiritual dimension, the ecstasy of communion. Communion is the ultimate freedom from the limitations of the self, the Small Mind and mundane sex. Opening yourself to this cosmic energy demands a moment-to-moment surrender into the fullness of the present moment. During sacred sex you identify with your lover, who has become merged with the divine. In this way the two of you become one, and in your oneness you are both part of the divine. The bliss that you offer then nourishes your very nature, so that you can experience and express more bliss in a self-perpetuating cycle.

Union as process

One of the insights of the Tantric tradition is that bliss is a process, and it is only through participating in this process that we really come to know bliss. Bliss is an evolving process that keeps unfolding, meaning that you need to keep making love in order to bring more bliss into being. An esoteric understanding of sacred sex is that this kind of conscious love-making is vitally important to sustain the dynamic charge of life, and that such love-making is like an offering to the erotic heart of the universe.

*Once you know how to merge into bliss, you experience more bliss,
and create more bliss each time you make love.*

Exercise:
The heart wave ritual

Build your sexual arousal

In this exercise, you create an energy connection with your beloved, in which you transfer loving, sexual energy to each other at the level of your genitals. You can sit on your partner's lap or do the exercise with your genitals physically connected. The energy swings between you in a U-shape, imaginatively connecting your sexual energy and your heart.

1 Start by connecting your heart and then igniting your sexual passion through breath and visualization.

2 Gaze into each other's eyes. Let the love build in your heart as you gaze at your beloved. Feel how you love and desire them.

3 Fall into slow, deep breathing together. Focus on imagining that you are drawing your breath up through your genitals with every in-breath, into your heart area. You may start with hand gestures to demonstrate to your partner where your breath is travelling, tracing the passage of the air as you imagine drawing it from your genitals up the front of your body to your heart, and then letting your hand drop as the breath goes down again.

4 Once you have settled into the same relaxed pace of breathing, fall into an alternate pattern of breathing, as one of you breathes out, your partner breathes in.

5 As your partner begins to inhale, release your breath, visualizing it dropping back down to your genitals. Imagine your breath streaming out of your genitals towards those of your partner and show him or her with your hand. Your partner then breathes in through his or her genitals and takes your breath up to his or her heart, incorporating sexual energy.

Exercise: Riding
the wave of bliss

1 Start with the previous exercise until you reach the point where you bring the sexual energy up to the heart. With each inhalation, draw the breath upward through the centre of your body, coming to rest in the area of your heart by the end of each inhalation. Next, start drawing the energy up to the crown of your head.

2 Move into the yab-yom (Shakti-Shiva) position where you are sitting upright with your legs wrapped around each other. Your genitals connect with penis to vulva, lying over the woman's clitoris, or man inside. The man concentrates on sending his energy out through his penis while the woman concentrates on receiving his loving energy.

3 The sexual energy gets more intense and builds higher with every breath, while your movements and breathing remain slow. Focus on your breathing, whether you are moving much or little; move the minimum amount required to maintain sexual excitement. Allow your pelvis to rock gently forward with each out-breath and backward with every in-breath. Imagine loving sexual energy streaming out. Receive and pull the energy up to the crown of your head.

4 When you join your mouths together, the energy recycles through the joined bodies. The woman breathes in through her genitals and out through her mouth, while the man inhales her precious breath and sends the energy downward and out through his genitals.

5 After 10 minutes of recycling breath, you may feel light headed. Breathe naturally, imagining circulating energy through your crown chakra, as you visualize yourselves enclosed in a ball of bliss.

6 Let the energy stream up your body and it will overflow over both of you, while you lose any sense of physical boundaries and rest in a field of bliss.

The afterglow: post-coital bliss

This is an important time for going deeper into your emotional and spiritual connection. After an experience of uniting and merging as one body, you have had a taste of what it is like to let go of your separate self and merge with something greater. According to Tantra, this is the ultimate nature of existence. The dimension of bliss is always there, if only you can tap into it. After making love, abandon yourself to the loving connectedness that is the lived experience of bliss.

Deepening the bliss

Post-coital meditation ensures that you remain deeply connected to your partner, even after the delights of love-making are over. Once bliss arises in you, you will discover that maintaining it is not dependent on

The crucible of your relationship can transform your sexual energies into ecstatic bliss – just as alchemists attempted to transform base metals into gold or raw materials into quintessence.

The Gnostic Lover

According to Gnostics, sex becomes a sacrament when you both surrender to longing for the divine, even at the risk of being burnt or consumed by the fire of such passion.

An esoteric metaphor of immolating one's self (the ego) on this transformative fire describes it as an offering to love. Complete surrender is only possible for a passionate lover. For Gnostics, such consuming love (longing) is necessary to enter into the mystery of sacred sex, which arises from the intimate knowledge born of deep love. In the language of gnosis, in the marriage chamber you are set on fire with the spirit of love – your self is completely consumed until only the Beloved remains.

Only a lover is truly a Gnostic – a knower – because it is only through the fruition of love that you find intimate knowledge (gnosis); the Gnostic can best be described as a passionate lover, for whom love is the fruit of sacred union.

external conditions. As you are in a very open mode during Tantric sex, this is the perfect moment in which to maximize your openness and encourage it to become part of your everyday reality.

During Tantric sex you will have already entered an altered state. Meditating afterwards either alone or with your partner, can help to consolidate that experience, and enable you to integrate it into your daily life.

Exercise: Imagine a field of loving energy

Living in bliss

Great sex opens you to bliss. You can use meditation to remain in bliss.
Maintain connection with your beloved to keep the bliss alive. Consolidate
your sexual connection by visualizing yourselves as part of each other.

1 In your post-orgasmic bliss, lie together with your heart wide open, full of love for your partner. It is important to remain physically close after orgasm, to deepen the bonding process. Leave the penis inside the vagina so that your love juices are mixed and energy blends.

2 Allow yourself to fall into a state of deep relaxation, without going to sleep. Alternatively, you may be in a state of non-thinking and emptiness or a state of bliss. Lie together, imagining that you are one united energy body. Cocoon your lover in your embrace.

3 Relax and deepen your breathing. Imagine your unified body wrapped in a ball of golden light. Breathe in as one body, exhale as one body.

4 Imagine that you are floating in the universal heart of your beloved, feeling deeply connected.

5 When you feel the love of the beloved flowing into you, you are in union. As long as you are still aware of the union, you have not fully surrendered and lost yourself. The message of sacred sex is to abandon yourself to love.

6 Once you become imbued with the divine through continual meditation and a sense of the sacred, the divine begins to manifest in you. You are no longer gazing into a secret mystery from the outside, but are inside it. This is the experience of divine illumination, or enlightenment.

Glossary

Active imagination: Focusing on an image while your mind freely associates in order to explore meaning.

Agape: Unconditional and compassionate love, which stems from the ability of the initiate to see the divine spark in all life.

Alchemy: Practical and philosophical pursuit of transforming base matter into spiritual essence.

Anima/Animus: Carl Jung defined the 'anima' as the feminine component of the unconscious male psyche and the 'animus' as the male component of the unconscious female psyche.

Bliss: Enlightenment (see below).

Buddha: Awakened one; a person who has achieved enlightenment. The historical Buddha is seen as an emanation of Buddha-nature, which underlies all phenomena.

Chakra ('wheel'): One of a series of focal points for the circulation of prana through the subtle body.

Dharma: Buddhist teachings describing the underlying order of the universe.

Duality: The polarization of existence into categories such as heaven and earth, spirit and matter masculine and feminine.

Ego: In Freudian and Jungian psychology, the conscious self; the individual part of the person.

Enlightenment: A state in which the self is liberated from the prison of materialism – the belief that we are matter and that

matter and spirit are divided; sustained awareness of the divine nature of reality.

Gnosticism: Judeo-Christian religious movement, swiftly branded heretical by the early Church, emphasizing the need for esoteric knowledge (or gnosis) of the divine.

Hermeticism: A religious movement attributed to Hermes Trigemistus, whose writings were a blend of Hellenic and Gnostic ideas about the divine.

Hieros gamos: Sexual ritual enacting the sacred marriage of the goddess and god, where humans represent the deities. Symbolically, it refers to the harmonization and unification of opposites.

Incubation: Meditating or sleeping in a sacred area in order to invite a dream or revelation from the spiritual realm.

Individuation: In Jungian terms, the gradual integration and unification of the Self through the resolution of layers of psychological conflict.

Karma: The impact of previous deeds (esp. in former lives) on one's current life; the law of cause and effect governing all action.

Kundalini: In yoga, a 'psycho-spiritual energy' – an instinctive or libidinal force – that lies coiled at the base of the spine waiting to be awakened. It rises through the chakras, producing spiritual knowledge and mystical powers.

Mantra: Sacred sound(s) for prayer; to evoke a particular deity.

Mindfulness: Conscious awareness.

Nirvana: State of release from the endless cycle of rebirth (samsara).

Prana: 'Breath', or spiritual essence, circulating around the subtle body. Similar concept to the Chinese chi.

Samsara: The cycle of birth, death and rebirth.

Self: In Freudian and Jungian psychology, the entire psyche, conscious and unconscious.

Shaivism: Hindu practice devoted to the worship of Shiva, creator, preserver and destroyer.

Shaktism: Hindu practices devoted to worship of the goddess or divine female power (Shakti, consort of Shiva). Often worshipped in fierce aspect, Kali.

Subtle body: System of channels and focal points within the human body around which prana/kundalini circulates.

Tantra: Esoteric traditions within Hinduism and Buddhism, pre-dating both. Rooted in goddess worship. Also: texts associated with these traditions.

Transpersonal: Term used by psychoanalysts for the spiritual.

Upanishads: Vedic texts written between 1000 and 500 BCE, which focus on philosophical and mystical questions rather than on gods and ritual.

Index

Figures in italics indicate captions
to photographs.

Index

Bibliography

Brauer Alan, and Donna, *ESO: How You and Your Lover Can Give Each Other Hours of Extended Sexual Orgasm*, Grand Central Publishing 2001

Brinton Perera, Sylvia, *Descent to the Goddess: A Way of Initiation for Women*, Inner City Books 1981

Cashford, Jules, Baring, Ann, *The Myth of the Goddess: Evolution of an Image*, Penguin 1993

Cook, Roger, *Tree of Life: Image for the Cosmos*, Thames and Hudson 1974

Chia, Mantak and Arava, Douglas, *The Multi-Orgasmic Man*, Harper One 1990

Fuerstein, Georg, *Tantra The Path of Ecstasy*, Shambhala 1998

Gimbutas, Marija, *The Civilization of the Goddess*, HarperSanFrancisco 1991

Jacobs, Alan, *The Essential Gnostic Gospels*, Watkins 2006

Kingsley, Peter, *Reality*, The Golden Sufi Center 2003

Lorius, Cassandra, *Tantric Sex: Making Love Last*, Thorsons 1999

Lorius, Cassandra, *The Tantric Pillow Book: 101 Nights of Sexual Ecstasy*, Harper Collins 2004

Mann, A.T. and Lyle, Jane, *Sacred Sexuality*, Element 1995

Mookerji, Ajit Kali; The Feminine Force Thames and Hudson 1988

Odier, Daniel, *Desire; The Tantric Path to Awakening*, Inner Traditions 2001

Osho and Shree Rajneeshpuram, Bhagwan, *Tantra Spirituality and Sex* 1983

Pagels, Elaine, *The Gnostic Gospel*, Vintage Books 1979

Pagels, Elaine, *Adam, Eve and the Serpent*, Vintage Books 1989

Porter, Roy, *Flesh in the Age of Reason*, Penguin 2003

Raff, Jeffrey, *The Wedding of Sophia*, Red Wheel/Weiser 2003

Ramsay Jay, *Crucible of Love*, O Books 2005

Ray, Reginald, *Secret of the Vajra World*, Shambhala 2002

Roob, Alexander, *Alchemy and Mysticism*, Taaschen 2006

Sarita, Ma Ananda, *Tantric Love: Journey into Sexual and Spiritual Ecstacy*, Gaia 2001

Shaw, Miranda, *Passionate Enlightenment; Women in Tantric Buddhism*, Princeton Paperbacks 1994

Showalter, Elaine, *The Female Malady: Women, Madness, and English Culture, 1830–1980*, Pantheon Books 1985

Urban, Hugh, *Tantra: Sex, Secrecy, Politics and Power in the Study of Religion*, University of California Press 2003

Welwood, John, *Perfect Love, Imperfect Relationships*, Shambhala 2006

Wilber, Ken, *Sex, Ecology, Spirituality: The Spirit of Evolution*, Shambhala 1995

Wolkstein, Diane, and Kramer, Samuel, *Inanna, Queen of Heaven and Earth*, Harper & Row 1983

Below is a list of websites which contain material of interest in contemporary sacred sex discussions:

For articles by Marnia Robinson and Gary Wilson see: www.reuniting.info/resources

Wave theory of matter: www.spaceandmotion.com

Walpola Rahula: www.buddhasociety.com

Mike Magee on *The Kali Yantra*: www.shivashakti.com

Peter and Maria Kingsley: 'As Far as Longing can Reach' www.peterkingsley.org

Lesley Hall on the history of sex in Victorian times www.lesleyahall.net

Gordon Rattray Taylor's book *Sex in History* is available online: www.ourcivilisation.com

The Crucible of Relationship www.johnwelwood.com

Acknowledgements

akg-images 44, 58; Francois Guenet 166; Gerard Degeorge 109; Gilles Mermet 56; IAM/World History Archive 82; Nimatallah 14; R & S Michaud 2, 200, 270; Ullstein Bild 188

Alamy Amar Grover/John Warburton-Lee Photography 237; Art Archive/Alfredo dagli Orti 120, 132; /Alfredo dagli Orti/Egyptian Museum; Cairo 40; /Gianni dagli Orti 19, 29, 97,122; Art Directors & TRIP 102; Butch Martin 172; Chris Hellier 50; Craig Lovell/Eagle Visions Photography 328; Dan O'Flynn 176; Dattatreya 246; Deborah Benbrook Photography 74; Dennis Cox 32; Fancy 358; Gianni Muratore 257; Image Source 379; Imagebroker 317; Interfoto 64, 70, 169, 269; Ivan Vdovin 93; John Glover 154; Maciej Wojtkowiak 307; Mary Evans Picture Library 27, 31, 76, 135; Nathan Benn 23; Peter Horree 18; Sherab 251, 273, 299; Tao Images Ltd 221, 252; The Art Gallery Collection 1, 43, 53, 60; The Print Collector 22, 45; Tomas Del Amo 149; Travel India 170; V & A Images 206; www.BibleLandPictures.com 77

Bridgeman Art Library Archives Charmet 277; British Library Board. All Rights Reserved 123; Dinodia 184; Osterreichische Nationalbibliothek; Vienna 54; Photo © Peter Nahum at The Leicester Galleries; London 49

Corbis AB/Susanne Borges 292; Alix Minde/PhotoAlto 165; Amanda Lynn/First Light 224; Amit Bhargava 278; Art Archive/Alfredo dagli Orti 114; Atlantide Phototravel 173; Beau Lark 190; Ben Welsh 287; Brigitte Sporrer 205; Bruce Talbot 209; Cedric Linn/Mind Body Soul 367; Christie's Images 129; Christophe Boisvieux 112; Courtesy of Museum of MEV/Ramon Manent 98; Earl & Nazima Kowall 216; Felix Wirth 360; Frédéric Soltan 17, 229; Gianni Dagli Orti 6; Godong/P Deliss 263; /Pascal Deloche 183; /Philippe Lissac 231; Heritage Images 85; Ingo Jezierski 249; Laura Doss 351; Lindsay Hebberd 264; Marcus Mok/Asia Images 340, 348; Massimo Listri 111; Mimmo Jodice 28; MM Productions 274; Ocean 239; Ole Graf 312; Onoky/A Chederros 178, /Nicolas Bets 354; Paul A Souders 267; Peter Aprahamian 143; Philadelphia Museum of Art 8; Red James 318; Roman Märzinger/Westend61 329

Dittrick Medical History Center Case Western Reserve University 127

Fotolia Beboy 65; Ed Lawrence 357; Frog 974 235; Ivan Trizlic 338; Jaroslav Machacek 207; Jurand 193; Just Sandeep 179; Karl Keller 375; Kati Molin 180; KaYann 217, 250; Kzenon 68; Laurent Hamels 78, 87, 291; Lily 303; Liping Dong 175; Lukas Hlavac 227; Masterlu 213; Maud Talèque 194; Microimages 386; Monkey Business 300; MORO 352; Ogressie 255; Paul Prescott 215; Pawel Kowalczyk 232; Perseomedusa 222; Piotr Marcinski 244; Vector Art Design 347; VG Studio 376; Videowokart 177; Yuri Arcurs 335

Getty Images Bill Derrick 138; Bridgeman Art Library 47, 119; Christoph Rosenberger 282, 381; Ciaran Griffin 242; DEA/Gianni dagli Orti 20; Don Emmert 67; Glow Images 147; Laurence Delderfield 72; Maria Teijeiro 158; Peter Willi 148; Ryan McVay 260; Suza Scalora 4

Mary Evans Picture Library 59, 145

Octopus Publishing Group John Davis 325;

Unit Photographic 285, 330, 333, 363, 368, 382, 384

Photolibrary Group Mirko Iannace 162; Photodisc 304

Photoshot De Agostini/World Illustrated 16

Picture Desk Art Archive/Eileen Tweedy 24; /Gianni dagli Orti/Egyptian Museum, Cairo 34, 35

Press Association Images David Cheskin/PA Archive 39

Foto Scala, Florence 61, 91

Science Photo Library 137, Asian and Middle Eastern Division/New York Public Library 214

SuperStock age fotostock 90, 187, 241; Blend Images 372; Corbis 198; Fine Art Photographic Library 103; Glow Wellness 218; Hemera 342; Huntington Library 81; Marka 161; Newberry Library, Chicago 101

Thinkstock 289; Creatas Images 94; Digital Vision 71; George Doyle 323; Getty Images 299; Goodshot 25, 36, 344, 364; Hemera 11, 21, 55, 99, 107, 141, 150, 152, 157, 297, 314; iStockphoto 86, 116, 210, 310, 336; Jupiterimages 202, 309, 320, 326; Photos.com 62; Pixland 7, 265; Stockbyte 346, 388

TopFoto Charles Walker 105, 125, 197, 201, 362, 370; Fortean 79; The British Library/HIP 63, 88; The Granger Collection 75, 112 left

Werner Forman Archive National Museum, Copenhagen 121; Private Collection 131; Theresa McCullough Collection, London 259

Additional decorative images from Fotolia and Thinkstock

The author is indebted to Jungian Julian David and his inspirational library, scholar Peter Kingsley for his gnostic dream interpretations and the many people who have brought the ideas in this book into common currency, making previously hidden, esoteric teachings available for any seeker. Thanks to those trail-blazers that mark out paths before us, so that we benefit from their experience and wisdom. Lastly thanks to the many tantra teachers who explore the sacred dimensions of sexuality in often innovative ways.

Commissioning Editor: Liz Dean
Editor: Jo Wilson
Copy Editor: Sarah Hoggett
Design: Tracy Killick Art Direction and Design
Art Direction: Yasia Williams-Leedham
Picture Researcher: Giulia Hetherington
Proofreader: Nicole Foster
Production: Lucy Carter
Indexer: Diana LeCore